GREAT
DISASTERS
OF THE 20th CENTURY

GREAT
DISASTERS
OF THE 20th CENTURY

Margot Keam Cleary

GALLERY BOOKS
An imprint of W.H. Smith Publishers Inc.
112 Madison Avenue
New York, New York 10016

Published by Gallery Books
A Division of W H Smith Publishers Inc.
112 Madison Avenue
New York, New York 10016

Produced by
Brompton Books Corp.
15 Sherwood Place
Greenwich, CT 06830

ISBN 0-8317-6920-3

Printed in Hong Kong

10 9 8 7 6 5 4 3 2 1

PAGE 1: *A Cincinnati resident is evacuated in the great flood of January, 1937, when enough rain fell along the Ohio Valley to put eight million acres under water and destroy 13,000 homes.*

PAGE 2: *A stand of trees bursts into flames in Wyoming's Grand Teton National Forest in August, 1988. Drought conditions fed the uncontrollable fires in the western United States, much like the fires that devastated Australia five years earlier.*

PAGE 3: *The violent eruption of Martinique's Mont Pelée on 1902 wiped out St. Pierre, a city of 30,000.*

THESE PAGES: *San Francisco residents displaced by the great earthquake of 1906 make do with salvaged possessions, and look out at the devastated city.*

Contents

Introduction

Although we may classify disasters as major or minor, great or small, to the person touched by calamity these distinctions are meaningless. The scale of disasters may vary, but the suffering they cause is the same. The anguish of the African women crying at the entrance to a Rhodesian mineshaft where 400 men are trapped is just as intense as the suffering in a city of a million rocked by an earthquake. Choosing the century's greatest disasters is a difficult task.

First, however, let us agree to take away the horrors inflicted purposely by man: war, genocide, terrorism. For our purposes a disaster must be unplanned, unpredictable, as if nature or technology had slipped from its usual limits. And let us also agree – perhaps more arbitrarily – to exclude such vast calamities as epidemics and famines. However lethal they may be, they nevertheless lack the focus and immediacy to qualify as disasters in quite the sense we mean.

Some disasters, like the sinking of the *Titanic* and the explosion of the *Hindenburg*, are legends by now, and standard on any list of great disasters. So are the huge natural disasters, the earthquakes, cyclones, floods that kill hundreds of thousands, even millions. Some man-made disasters, like the fire in New York's Triangle Shirtwaist Factory, deserve to be included because they served as a catalyst for change afterwards. And it's important to examine the new disasters that twentieth-century technology has unwittingly ushered in: the oil spill from a supertanker, the spacecraft that explodes, the radiation leak from a nuclear reactor.

ABOVE: *The* Challenger *space shuttle explodes over Cape Canaveral on January 28, 1986.*

BELOW: *After Hurricane Hugo made its way through the Caribbean in 1989, residents of St.* Croix, *wait in line for water at a gasoline station.*

RIGHT: *A raging forest fire makes its way toward Yellowstone National Park's Old Faithful complex, September 7, 1988.*

But looking only at thousands of deaths and millions of dollars in damages can be numbing. Often it's the smaller disasters that remind us most acutely of what they mean in human terms. We see the faces of the fans crushed to death at a British soccer match, or listen to the words of a little boy in Wales who has seen his friends disappear under an avalanche of mud.

In the end, all disasters, large and small, serve a common purpose. They remind us just how fragile our world really is. It is, however, heartening to reflect that times of disaster can also reveal more worthwhile qualities. When Iran was struck by a devastating earthquake in June 1990, aid was immediately offered by dozens of countries, including many who were otherwise opposed to Iran's rulers and their policies. The hope brought by such co-operations may be the true lesson to be learned from this book.

LEFT: *A woman in black makes her way through the ruins of San Francisco, after much of the city was destroyed by the great earthquake of April 18, 1906, and the subsequent fires. Between 700 and 3000 people died, and 300,000 were left homeless, in this disaster.*

RIGHT: *A boy gazes in shock after an avalanche caused by the 1985 eruption of Colombia's Nevado del Ruiz virtually wiped out his town and its 20,000 inhabitants.*

BELOW: *A disaster that became legendary: the sinking of the* Titanic.

The Galveston Hurricane – 1900

Galveston, Texas, was a city on its way up as the twentieth century began. Set on a sand bar in the gleaming Gulf of Mexico just off the Texas mainland, Galveston had a booming shipping industry that had turned it into the fourth wealthiest city, per capita, in the United States. Times were good.

So good, in fact, that when trouble arrived, many Galvestonians reacted by burying their heads in the sand. Early on the morning of September 8, 1900, when a storm descended on the city, nobody paid it much mind. Galveston, they figured, had weathered storms before: why not again? Some people even whiled away the morning on the beach, admiring the rising wind and waves.

But to serious weather-watchers this was no ordinary storm. The barometer fell to 29 inches, then to 28.5. Increasing gusts drove the pelting rain almost horizontally. Then Galveston's reliable northerly wind, which countered the force of most storms from the southeast, suddenly vanished and left the city defenseless against what was by now a hurricane.

Even then most people didn't worry. A weather service employee who rode down to the beach on horseback to issue warnings was largely ignored. By evening it was too late for warnings.

The rain poured down. The wind rose to 85 miles per hour. The editor of the local paper recounted the scene like this: "To go out upon the streets was to court death. Cisterns, portions of buildings, telegraph poles, walls were falling, and the noise of the wind and the crashing of buildings was terrifying in the extreme. The people were like rats in a trap." Just after 7:30 PM a tidal wave driven by the storm washed over the city to destroy what wind and rain had not yet claimed.

People who had refused to leave their cottages on the shore were washed out to sea or were crushed when their homes fell in on them. Others drifted about on scraps of wood or bales of hay for hours before succumbing to the flood waters. Three of Galveston's most prominent citizens were among the first to die: they had just raised their glasses in a carefree toast to the storm in one of the city's taverns when the roof collapsed, killing them all. Every one of the residents of the city's Old Women's Home perished, as did all but two of the hundred or so children at the orphanage run by the Sisters of Charity, despite the sisters' heroic attempts to save them by tying the children to their waists. Rescuers came upon the pathetic sight of small clusters of children linked to their would-be saviors by a thin rope.

LEFT: *Much of Galveston, Texas, was levelled by wind and water in the devastating hurricane of 1900. The school in the foreground was carried 600 feet by the flood waters after a tidal wave swamped the city.*

BELOW: *In the aftermath of Galveston's hurricane, local militia aid the relief efforts.*

ABOVE: *Although the destruction caused by the 1915 hurricane in Galveston was mild compared with the 1900 hurricane, it was enough to strand this boat on a railroad track.*

RIGHT: *Galveston's stunned survivors pick through the wreckage. The death toll would eventually stand at 6000.*

The efforts of another group of nuns, however, did succeed. The sturdy Ursuline Convent, not far from the beach, was flooded to the second floor, but that did not prevent the sisters from fishing nearly a thousand people from the water with ropes and poles.

Over 6000 people died in the Galveston hurricane, making it the most deadly natural disaster in United States history. The city was left in ruins, a third of it washed away and most of the rest a mass of broken buildings. Victims of the storm lay everywhere, a scene made even more gruesome by the thousands of coffins that had washed from Galveston's shallow graves.

In the space of one day, Galveston had seen its population decimated and its buildings reduced to rubble. But the city's optimistic spirit survived, and "Galveston shall rise again!" became a rallying cry. Galveston had learned its lesson, however. The rebuilt city included a seawall 11 miles long and nearly 20 feet high. When the next big hurricane struck, in 1915, the city was again battered by high winds and water, but this time, Galveston made it through.

The Eruption of Mont Pelée – 1902

With its pastel houses, green plantations and a sparkling sea capped by a bright blue sky, the city of St. Pierre on Martinique was one of the jewels of the Caribbean, a cosmopolitan blend of Western and native cultures. But it sat just beneath an ominous reminder of nature's darker side: a 4430-foot volcano, Mont Pelée.

Yet the citzens of St. Pierre gave little thought to Pelée's power. Although it had erupted twice just a half century earlier, many considered Pelée to be dormant. And so in April of 1902 when the volcano began to rumble, then to throw off showers of ash, the city remained generally serene. The rumbling turned to hissing and the showers of ash became so dense that they darkened the sky. Downpours of rain then mixed with the heavy ash, and soon the smell of sulfur in the air was so strong that horses began to drop in the streets. Mud avalanches and volcanic debris began to clog the city. Despite all this, both political and church leaders in the city continued to assure its citizens that the worst was over. On May 8 they were proven wrong.

Just before 8:00 that morning, Pelée erupted with a violent explosion, flames shooting from its crater. At the same time, the side of the volcano burst open with a roar, spewing forth lava, ash and incandescent gas that bore down on the city below. The destruction was devastating and instantaneous. In three minutes virtually the entire population of St. Pierre was gone. Some victims were burned to death by the boiling lava; others were buried by the thick mud when ash mixed with the morning's torrential rains. In St. Pierre's harbor 16 ships that had been riding at achor were capsized by the river of lava flowing into the sea, and their crews were boiled alive. But most victims died instantly, immolated by the superheated cloud of steam and gas that shot from Pelée. *Nuee ardente*, it was called – "glowing cloud."

Within hours the French had sent troops in on a rescue mission, but the task was futile: of St. Pierre's 30,000 people only four had survived the blast, and three of them died soon after. The one man who did live – a convicted murderer whose identity remains a source of confusion to historians – had watched Pelée's onslaught through a tiny crack in the window of his basement jail cell. The would-be rescuers could only turn to the monumental task of burying the thousands of victims.

Mont Pelée erupted four more times in 1902. The last eruption, on August 20, killed another 2000, many of them people who had come to help bury the dead and rebuild the city. In all, the 1902 eruptions of Mont Pelée claimed more than 40,000 lives.

The rest of Martinique was barely touched by Pelée; the volcano's destruction had been confined to the area on which its "glowing cloud" settled and the path that its river of lava made on its way to the sea. But in 1902 Mont Pelée worked such devastation, in so little time, that it has become the standard by which all other volcanic disasters are judged.

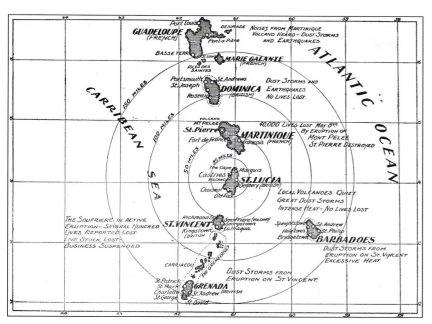

ABOVE: *This chart illustrates the effects of the 1902 volcanic activity on nearby islands. Noises and dust storms from Mt. Pelée's eruption were experienced 100 miles away.*

ABOVE RIGHT: *A ruined church stands among the rubble of Martinique's St. Pierre after the city was wiped out by Mont Pelée's eruption on May 8, 1902. Molten lava, mud avalanches and searing heat took their toll on the population of 30,000, of which only one survived.*

RIGHT: *A rare photo depicts the superheated cloud of ash and gas that issued from the eruption of Mont Pelée.*

LEFT: *A desolate view of St. Pierre, looking toward the bay. The picturesque city became a wasteland within minutes of the massive eruption.*

The Iroquois Theatre Fire – 1903

In 1903 the Iroquois was Chicago's newest and biggest theatre, as well as "absolutely fireproof" – or so its program proudly proclaimed. But little more than a month after its opening it was in ashes.

The matinee performance of *Mr. Bluebeard* on December 30 had drawn a standing room-only audience of 1830, mostly mothers and children on a holiday outing to see the latest pantomime from England. The first act was just concluding with a rendition of "In the Pale Moonlight" when stagehands noticed that the lamp that provided the "moonlight" had ignited a bit of scenery above the stage. One man tried to put it out with his hands, another with a stick. When those attempts failed, they aimed a fire extinguisher at the flames, but only a useless powder sprayed from it.

By now members of the audience were beginning to notice flames shooting from around the thickly painted scenery. Comic Eddie Foy, the star of the show, appeared on stage to try to calm the theatre-goers. Half in, half out of his costume, with a red wig atop his head, he turned to the orchestra. "Play!" he urged the musicians. "Start an overture, start anything. But play!" Stay calm, Foy told the audience, and leave in an orderly fashion.

Coupled with the reassuring music, Foy's words had their effect – on those who could hear him. People seated in the front of the theatre left their seats quietly. But Foy's voice hadn't carried up to the balcony, and people seated there were growing increasingly anxious. When an open stage door let in a sudden gust of wind that fanned the fire out onto the stage and into the seats, they panicked.

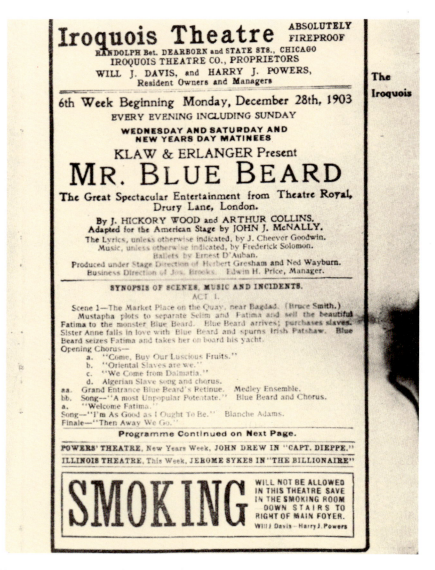

Burning scenery began cascading down onto the stage. Then the electricity went out and plunged the theatre into darkness, save for the ribbon of flame that was making its way along the ceiling. Crowds began rushing for the exits, only to find them locked, frozen or rusted shut. Dozens more following behind trampled those in front. People who headed for the fire escapes fared no better, trapped when they discovered that some lacked ladders and that the ladders of others were slick with ice. In the meantime the theatre filled with smoke.

Not all the escape routes were dead ends, however. Painters working on a building next door laid out a plank over which a handful of people crawled to safety. An elevator operator backstage ran his lift again and again to bring down performers stranded at the stage's aerial level, not stopping until the control box caught fire and brought the elevator to a halt. Another man led 50 stagehands trapped below the stage to a coal hole and stood guard until they escaped.

Chicago firefighters had the blaze under control within minutes of their arrival at the theatre – but by then it was too late. When the bodies were counted, 602 people had died in the Iroquois Theatre blaze. Two hundred of them were claimed by fire in the first minutes, and the rest had been crushed in the panic that followed.

The tragedy hit Chicago hard. Although an attempt to try the theatre management and city officials for manslaughter amounted to nothing, change was underway. The worst theatre fire in United States history set the stage for the nation's first fire code for public buildings.

OPPOSITE TOP: *A charred program for the ill-fated Iroquois Theatre production,* Mr. Bluebeard, *retrieved from the fire that claimed 602 lives on December 30, 1903.*

OPPOSITE BOTTOM: *A view from the stage of the Iroquois Theatre reveals an auditorium scorched by fire and damaged by the crush of people trying to escape.*

BELOW: *The scene in front of the theatre during the fire, as victims are being carried out. Ambulances, doctors and nurses from all over Chicago hurried to the aid of the injured and dying.*

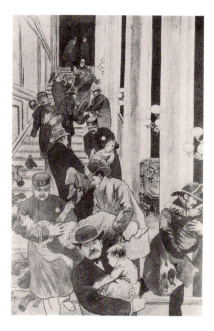

ABOVE: *A depiction of frenzied activity at the theatre, as rescue workers attempt to remove bodies and treat survivors. Only a third of the deaths were burn victims; the rest succumbed to smoke inhalation and the panicked crush to escape.*

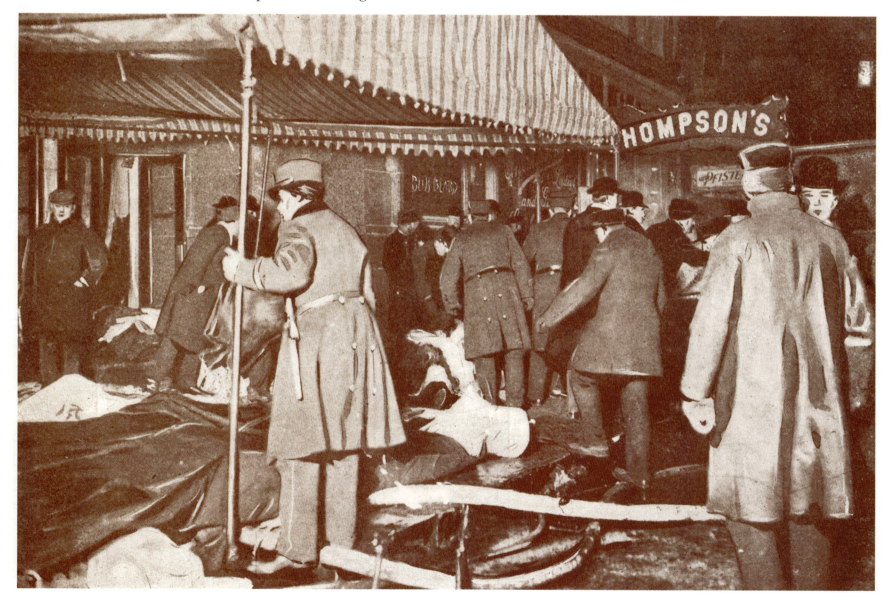

The Sinking of the *General Slocum* – 1904

Spirits were high as the excursion steamer *General Slocum* pulled away from the pier in New York City on the morning of June 15, 1904. The families of St. Mark's German Lutheran Church were setting off on their annual picnic. Mothers chatted as they watched their children run about the decks.

An hour later, the good cheer was gone. "Fire!" a woman shouted, and the picnickers looked up to see flames shooting from the front of the ship. Despite fresh paint, the *General Slocum* was in sad repair, and the fire spread quickly through its old wooden hull. The crew knew little of firefighting, and in any case, the fire hoses didn't work.

Mothers gathered up their children and headed toward the stern of the ship, away from the flames. But then the captain, William Van Schaick, did a foolish thing: instead of steering toward the Manhattan shore, just 300 yards away, he headed for a less populated island upriver. As the ship steamed on, the wind she created fanned the flames and sent them aft, directly into the midst of the huddled families.

Van Schaick finally put his ship ashore on North Brother Island, but he missed the beach and crashed onto rocks, making escape from the burning vessel nearly impossible for most of the terrified passengers. Van Schaick himself lost no time in leaping onto a tugboat that had come to the rescue, and most of his crew followed suit, leaving the passengers to fend for themselves.

A few people managed to grab lifejackets, but the vests were useless, filled with sawdust and weighted down so that they would pass inspection. Lifeboats were wired into place. As the flames spread throughout the *General Slocum* and the heat grew unbearable, passengers began to jump overboard. Most, unable to swim, drowned. Others were pulled down into the river by the ship's paddlewheel, which continued to turn.

Captain and crew may have abandoned ship, but heroes did emerge from the tragedy. To their credit, the *General Slocum's* two engineers stayed at their posts (one later died in the water), along with one lone crewman who gathered up passengers and carried them to shore.

The river was filled with the horns of fireboats and tugs heading toward the *General Slocum* at full speed. Crewmen from some of the tugs jumped into the river to rescue infants tossed down by desperate mothers. One policeman managed to carry 11 children to shore before drowning in his attempt to save a twelfth. A nurse from a hospital on the island couldn't swim but still managed to pull many children from the river. A patient at the same hospital waded in up to her neck and was able to rescue 20 people.

For his role in the *General Slocum* tragedy Captain Van Schaick was convicted of manslaughter and sentenced to 10 years in prison; in 1908 he was pardoned by President Theodore Roosevelt because of advanced age. But his poor seamanship and cowardice had left over 1000 dead and New York's East Side devastated. For months families sustained the hope that their loved ones had somehow escaped death, and now and then touching reminders of the *General Slocum* disaster would turn up in the city papers. A family would publish a photograph of its child with the question, "Have you seen this little girl?" No missing child ever turned up.

RIGHT: *Relief workers retrieve bodies from New York's East River after the tragic fire aboard the* General Slocum *claimed 1000 lives. The extent of the disaster was greatly exacerbated by poor judgment by the ship's captain, who was later convicted of manslaughter due to his role in the awful incident.*

FAR RIGHT, BELOW: *Twisted metal work on the* General Slocum's *main deck illustrates the effect of the terrific heat generated by the fire. Because of ineffective lifesaving equipment, only 400 people were saved from the pleasure boat.*

BELOW: *The* General Slocum, *moored at dockside, after her disastrous outing on June 15, 1904.*

The San Francisco Earthquake – 1906

As events in 1989 reminded the world, California is earthquake country. Set on top of the shifting plates of the San Andreas Fault, the state is always poised for yet another tremor that rattles the dishes and sends children scrambling under their school desks. But it was one great earthquake at the turn of the century that firmly linked California and earthquakes in the public's mind.

Most of San Francisco was sleeping on the morning of April 18, 1906, when a terrifying 40-second shock at 5:13 jolted it awake. Ten seconds later, another shock rocked the city. Fissures in the earth opened and closed, and the pavement undulated in sickening waves. As their homes began to crumble and shower debris on them, hundreds of people headed for the streets.

The pride of San Francisco, the new city hall specifically designed to withstand earthquakes, did not withstand this one; when the quake was over, only the building's domed tower of steel was still standing. Streetcar tracks were bent grotesquely out of shape, and many of the buildings that had not collapsed tilted crazily. Below street level another part of San Francisco was splitting apart: the city's gas and electric lines. From the broken lines sprang a fire that would flatten much of the city and compound the disaster.

As fires spread, up to 75,000 people fled by ferryboat and on foot. Everywhere gas was igniting. One woman lit a match in her kitchen and set off an explosion that eventually leveled hundreds of homes. An eyewitness to the fires said they blazed like volcanoes in the streets, and the flames could be seen from 50 miles away.

All through the day the fire continued to burn. Water mains, too, had burst, leaving the San Francisco fire department almost helpless to battle the blaze. Adding to the gravity of the situation was the fact that the fire chief had been an early victim of the quake, crushed when the chimney of his home collapsed. In the marine district of the city people fetched buckets of water from the bay to fight the fire's onslaught.

In a last-ditch effort to halt the fire's progress by blasting away everything in its path, the mayor authorized the dynamiting of the city. The late fire chief had included dynamited firebreaks in a plan he had worked out for dealing with a major conflagration in San Francisco. But, without the Chief there to oversee the work, the job was botched, and the so-called firebreaks accomplished little. The fire continued to skip through the city, propelled by the wind currents it created. It was not until the next day that more dynamiting succeeded in halting the major rush of flames.

When the fire was finally extinguished three days later, San Francisco lay in ruins: twisted and broken by the earthquake, scorched by the fire. Most estimates say that more than 700 people died from the combined quake and fire. (A study published in 1990, however, claims to have found documented proof of at least 3000 deaths.) Over 500 city blocks, three quarters of the city, were destroyed, and 300,000 people were homeless. Property damage approached half a billion dollars.

News coverage of the 1989 earthquake in San Francisco gave it an immediacy missing from accounts of the earlier quake. But that has not diminished the reputation of the 1906 disaster; to most people it will remain *the* Great San Francisco Earthquake.

TOP LEFT: *A view up a residential San Francisco street shows the effects of the 1906 earthquake: the ground heaved aside cobblestones, twisted trolley tracks and shattered the sidewalk.*

LEFT: *Troops patrol Market Street while San Francisco still burns from the fires that followed her most devastating earthquake.*

TOP: *Wary of aftershocks, a family dines outdoors in the aftermath of the great earthquake, on Franklin Street near Fulton. Across the street much of the city has been flattened.*

ABOVE: *A horse-drawn fire engine races to battle blazes caused by exploding gas lines after the earthquake.*

ABOVE LEFT: *A hastily erected camp in San Francisco's Jefferson Square houses refugees from the great earthquake, and those whose homes are intact but in danger of falling.*

LEFT: *In contrast to the photo above it, this view depicts campers before a modern skyline after San Francisco's earthquake of October 17, 1989.*

ABOVE: *Oakland Athletic and San Francisco Giant players and their families on the field at Candlestick Park after the earthquake brought to a temporary halt the cross-bay World Series of 1989.*

RIGHT: *Workmen on the quake-damaged section of Oakland's Bay Bridge hook up a crane to lift the collapsed sections on October 22, 1989.*

The Messina Earthquake – 1908

The people of Messina, on the Mediterranean island of Sicily, had lived with earthquakes for centuries. Back in 1783, 60,000 of its people had been killed in one, and in the years leading up to 1908 the city had grown accustomed to tremors. Repairing the stone buildings damaged by shocks had become almost routine in Messina.

Just before dawn on the morning of December 28, 1908, a brief tremor woke the city. It was followed by another shock of perhaps 10 seconds. Then the city was hit by a succession of tremors of such duration – 30 to 40 seconds – and such violence that Messina simply fell to the ground. In the space of minutes 98 percent of the city was obliterated.

Thousands of people rushed into the streets to escape the heavy stone structures that were crumbling around them. Everywhere the ground was splitting open, swallowing people and buildings. Said one survivor later, "The earth seemed suddenly to drop and then to turn violently on its axis. The whole population, precipitated from their houses rent in twain, were spun around like tops as they ran through the streets." Gas pipes broke, starting fires throughout the city.

With the quake came torrential rains and high winds that made the scene even more horrific. And finally, with the earth heaving and the skies opening up, the sea had its turn too, drawing back from the shore and then returning in the form of a 40-foot wave that thundered in with incredible speed, destroying everything in its path. The Strait of Messina, which separated Sicily from Italy, became almost unrecognizable, stripped of the landmarks and lighthouses on which sailors relied for navigation.

Thousands of people in Messina were buried alive under buildings. Some were rescued, only to perish later or go mad from what they had endured. Victims trapped

TOP: *An artist's engraving depicts the chaos and destruction visited upon Messina by an earlier earthquake in 1783.*

ABOVE: *A view of Messina's devastated waterfront a few days after the earthquake of 1908. Collapsing buildings and a 40-foot tidal wave claimed 80,000 lives.*

LEFT: *A makeshift emergency surgical station in Messina after the 1908 earthquake, where doctors attempt to treat victims with what resources they could gather.*

for days were crazed by pain and hunger, and some were even driven to gnawing on the bodies of the dead. One rescuer discovered a family of five children pinned under their house, clinging to their dead mother's body. The children were left mute from the experience. Another man staged a grotesque song and dance on the docks, seemingly oblivious to the dead child he held in his arms. Said a soldier who took in all that happened, "Dante's *Inferno* gives but a faint idea of what happened at Messina . . . the streets blocked by fallen horses. Balconies, chimneys, bell towers, entire walls had been thrown down. From every side arose the screams and moans of the wounded."

Within days huge funeral pyres were lighting up the sky above Sicily as survivors burned the bodies of the dead. The toll in Messina alone was 80,000, more than half the population. But the earthquake had not confined itself to Sicily; it had reached out for 120 miles in all directions and devastated much of the Italian mainland. In Reggio di Calabria, a city of 34,000 on the other side of the Strait of Messina, 25,000 people were killed. When the victims in the surrounding villages were added to the casualty figures, the Messina earthquake of 1908 may have claimed as many as 160,000 lives.

The Triangle Shirtwaist Factory Fire – 1911

Another long week's work was almost over at the Triangle Shirtwaist Factory in New York City. It was Saturday, March 25, 1911, and the young immigrant women squeezed behind row upon row of sewing machines on the top three floors of the 10-story building were getting ready to leave for the day.

Then, in the eighth-floor cutting room, fire broke out in a pile of rags. The building itself had been pronounced fireproof in the press, but the rows of shirts hanging from the ceiling and scraps of fabric on the floor certainly were not, and the fire engulfed the eighth floor and then spread upwards.

Most of the people on the top floor managed to escape to the roof, but those on the lower two floors were not so lucky. To prevent pilferage of shirts, the owners of the factory had installed narrow exits through which all workers had to pass for inspection. In the rush to escape the fire panic-stricken girls on the eighth and ninth floors of the factory soon jammed those exits. Other doors were locked, and the stairwells quickly filled with flames. For a while, the elevator provided an escape route for some, but soon the intense heat damaged the cables and put it out of commission. Desperate women jumped into the shaft and were killed when they crashed onto the top of the elevator far below.

Others made their way to the fire escape, only to find that it offered no way out; the ladder had never been completed and ended far above the pavement. Girls got to the bottom of the escape ladder and stopped dead, afraid to jump. But more girls were following behind, and soon the metal ladder collapsed under their combined weight. They all fell to their deaths on the concrete below.

Firefighters had responded to the blaze in minutes, but neither their ladders nor the water from their hoses could reach the building's upper stories. Girls crowded into the windows, some tearing their hair as they realized the choice they faced. The firemen watched helplessly as one girl after another approached the windows and then leaped when the heat and flames became unbearable. Others were pushed by girls behind them struggling toward the windows for a breath of fresh air. Rescuers held out life nets and sheets of canvas to try to catch the girls as they jumped, but the force of the falls made the effort useless: bodies tore holes in the nets and crashed to the pavement. Many of the girls linked arms with friends and tumbled down in clusters of three or four.

Firefighters put out the fire in just 18 minutes. But by that time it had claimed 145, almost all young women. More than 20 bodies were found in the elevator shaft, and 50 in front of a jammed ninth-floor door.

Public outrage over the loss of life focused on conditions at the shirtwaist factory: workers packed in with little room to move, doors that opened in instead of out, inadequate staircases and fire escapes. The lack of exits had been noted in a fire department report to the city, but no action had been taken.

A mass funeral for the victims drew over 100,000 mourners, many from the city's new labor unions. For years to come unions fighting for better working conditions would point to the Triangle Factory as an example of all that was wrong with worker safety. In the end, the tragedy of the Triangle Shirtwaist Factory fire helped to produce some notable victories for the American labor movement: more stringent fire and safety codes, and even the eventual demise of the notorious sweatshop system itself.

RIGHT: *It took firefighters less than 20 minutes to douse the deadly blaze at New York City's Triangle Shirtwaist Factory on March 25, 1911. But because of the lack of exits, crowded working conditions, inadequate staircases and fire escapes, and doors that opened in instead of out, the fire claimed 145 young lives.*

BELOW LEFT: *Charred lumber and machinery were all that remained on many floors of the Triangle Shirtwaist Factory after the scorching fire.*

BELOW: *Next of kin have the gruesome task of identifying bodies of victims from the fire. Translating public outrage into concern, over 100,000 mourners – many from the city's new labor unions – attended the mass funeral.*

The Sinking of the *Titanic* – 1912

As she set out from England in April of 1912 on her maiden voyage to New York, everything about the *Titanic* was steeped in glamour. She boasted luxurious fittings: a theatre, a tennis court, four dining rooms, even a miniature golf course. She had a double bottom and series of watertight compartments that made her unsinkable, according to her owners, the White Star Line. And her first crossing had attracted a passenger list that read like *Who's Who*. John Jacob Astor was on board, as were Isidor Straus, founder of Macy's department store, and Colonel Washington Roebling, designer of the Brooklyn Bridge.

The *Titanic* was four days into her journey across the Atlantic when she began receiving word by radio that icebergs, loosened from the polar cap by warm weather, were floating south into shipping lanes. On the evening of April 14 the radio operator took down yet another such warning from a ship just ahead of the *Titanic*. "Saw much heavy ice pack and great number large icebergs." The radio operator set the message aside until he had time to send it to the bridge.

He would never get the chance. Just before midnight the lookout sighted a tremendous mass of ice rising out of the water on the *Titanic's* starboard bow. The call went to the bridge: "Iceberg right ahead!"

The crew struggled to turn the ship from her collision course with the iceberg, but both were moving too fast. A 300-foot length of the *Titanic* scraped up hard against the iceberg.

Captain Edward Smith ordered the ship's watertight compartments shut. But within an hour it was clear that they were not watertight; the *Titanic* was taking on water and beginning to list. The captain sent stewards from cabin to cabin to request that passengers head for the lifeboats. On the upper decks most people refused to believe that the minor jolt they had felt was cause for alarm, but water was rising in the steerage section, and passengers there were already growing frantic.

Soon after midnight the *Titanic* sent out distress signals and shot off flares, which were inexplicably ignored by a ship just 10 miles away. By now Captain Smith had ordered passengers into the lifeboats. Many, feeling secure on the huge ship on calm seas, refused to go, and some

OPPOSITE: A drawing depicts the sinking of the Titanic *in the early morning hours of April 15, 1912.*

RIGHT: The day after the disaster, The New York Times *reported all that was known of the* Titanic's *demise, including a partial list of the saved.*

BELOW: This rare photo shows a lifeboat from the Titanic *alongside the* Carpathia, *which picked up the 705 survivors; 1502 people perished with the* Titanic.

"All the News That's Fit to Print."

The New York Times.

THE WEATHER.

VOL. LXI...NO. 19,806. NEW YORK, TUESDAY, APRIL 16, 1912.—TWENTY-FOUR PAGES. ONE CENT

TITANIC SINKS FOUR HOURS AFTER HITTING ICEBERG; 866 RESCUED BY CARPATHIA, PROBABLY 1250 PERISH; ISMAY SAFE, MRS. ASTOR MAYBE, NOTED NAMES MISSING

Col. Astor and Bride, Isidor Straus and Wife, and Maj. Butt Aboard.

"RULE OF SEA" FOLLOWED

Women and Children Put Over in Lifeboats and Are Supposed to be Safe on Carpathia.

PICKED UP AFTER 8 HOURS

Vincent Astor Calls at White Star Office for News of His Father and Leaves Weeping.

FRANKLIN HOPEFUL ALL DAY

Manager of the Line Insisted Titanic Was Unsinkable Even After She Had Gone Down.

HEAD OF THE LINE ABOARD

J. Bruce Ismay Making First Trip on Gigantic Ship That Was to Surpass All Others.

The Lost Titanic Being Towed Out of Belfast Harbor.

CAPT. E. J. SMITH, Commander of the Titanic.

PARTIAL LIST OF THE SAVED.

Includes Bruce Ismay, Mrs. Widener, Mrs. H. B. Harris, and an Incomplete name, suggesting Mrs. Astor's.

Biggest Liner Plunges to the Bottom at 2:20 A.M.

RESCUERS THERE TOO LATE

Except to Pick Up the Few Hundreds Who Took to the Lifeboats.

WOMEN AND CHILDREN FIRST

Cunarder Carpathia Rushing to New York with the Survivors.

SEA SEARCH FOR OTHERS

The California Stands By on Chance of Picking Up Other Boats or Rafts.

OLYMPIC SENDS THE NEWS

Only Ship to Flash Wireless Messages to Shore After the Disaster.

---

boats put off only partly filled. Then, as the *Titanic* listed more and it became impossible to lower the lifeboats on the port side, a terrifying fact began to dawn on those who remained on board: the ship was indeed sinking, and they were going to go down with it.

As the *Titanic*'s stern began to rise out of the water the sailors manning the lifeboats rowed frantically to get clear. At 2:20 AM the ship's boilers exploded, sending her innards forward with a great shudder. In moments the *Titanic* was standing nearly straight out of the water, flinging all on deck into the ocean before the ship itself slipped out of sight.

Just over 1500 passengers and crew out of 2207 on board were lost with the *Titanic*. At 4:00 that morning the *Carpathia*, which had been making full speed for the *Titanic* despite the danger of icebergs, came upon her lifeboats adrift in the ocean.

At the New York office of the White Star Line, officials reassured the press for hours that the delayed liner was experiencing only minor problems. Only when word came from the *Carpathia* that she had picked up survivors did the White Star Line concede that the impossible had happened.

The *Titanic* remained undisturbed on the bottom of the ocean for nearly three-quarters of a century. In 1985 a French-American team located her and brought back thousands of photographs to a world still intrigued by the *Titanic*'s story. On one of its dives, the team placed a plaque on the liner's stern that read, "In memory of those souls who perished with the *Titanic*, April 14/15, 1912."

The Halifax Explosion – 1917

When it sailed into Halifax, Nova Scotia, on the morning of December 6, 1917, the French steamship *Mont Blanc*, fresh from New York, was a floating bomb, laden with thousands of tons of explosives headed for the war in Europe. The ship had stopped over in Halifax to await convoy protection for its precious cargo. But the explosives would do their damage far from the front.

As the *Mont Blanc* eased into the harbor the Belgian ship *Imo* was coming out, empty except for its ballast. Closing in on one another, the two ships sounded a series of whistle blasts to signal their intentions, but somehow the signals were not properly understood, and what had a moment before been approaching courses suddenly became collision courses.

The *Mont Blanc's* captain knew that this could be no ordinary collision. With his volatile cargo, an explosion was almost inevitable. He tried to position the *Mont Blanc* so that the *Imo* would strike it at the least vulnerable spot. But it was little use, and moments later the *Imo* sliced into the *Mont Blanc's* side. Barrels filled with benzene spilled open and cascaded onto explosives, setting off a roaring fire.

Accounts of the crew's actions vary. Some say they valiantly battled the blaze before finally abandoning ship to row furiously to shore. Others say they tore from the *Mont Blanc* immediately. No matter, for once the fire had started there was no chance of putting it out. Seventeen minutes after the collision Halifax was wracked by an explosion of such magnitude that it was heard 60 miles away.

The *Mont Blanc* disappeared in an instant. The *Imo*, which had been able to make for shore despite the collision, was lifted from the water and thrown onto land. The crews of other ships in the harbor were killed by the force

ABOVE: *A photo taken after the 1917 explosion of the* Mont Blanc *in Nova Scotia's Halifax Harbor reveals the extent to which the waterfront was leveled by the blast. The explosion, together with the tidal wave, fires and collapsing buildings that followed, claimed more than 1600 lives.*

LEFT: *Some search the ruins of a shattered house while others numbly look on, after the Halifax explosion. At least 3000 homes were destroyed in the disaster.*

RIGHT: *Halifax rebuilds after the disastrous explosion. Reconstruction efforts were aided by the support of Nova Scotia's neighbors.*

of the explosion, and hundreds of dock workers drowned when a tidal wave triggered by the blast swamped the waterfront. Buildings were rocked from their foundations and hundreds of children were killed when their schools caved in. Other munitions stored onshore exploded, and fires tore through the city.

Power lines, cables and transportation were all destroyed. Just one telegraph line remained over which Halifax could call for help. The operator remained on the job for 20 minutes, then abandoned his post when he learned that his wife was on her deathbed.

More than 1600 people died as a result of the Halifax explosion and the tidal wave and fires that followed. Another 8000 were injured. In the space of minutes 3000 homes were gone.

The explosion brought an outpouring of support from Halifax' neighbors. Scores of doctors and nurses descended on the city. The US Navy sent 50,000 blankets to help the homeless ward off the numbing cold. The State of Maine shipped 400,000 feet of lumber and 200,000 panes of glass to aid in the recovery effort. The city soon rallied, but the Halifax disaster probably remains the most deadly accidental explosion of the century.

Mention must be made of another, strikingly similar disaster that occurred in Bombay harbor in February, 1944, when the British ammunition ship *Fort Stikine* blew up as a result of an accidental fire in one of its holds. Once again, the devastation visited on the port and on other ships in the harbor (27 were sunk or destroyed) was immense. And although it is generally thought that the death toll in Halifax was higher, there is just enough doubt about this to warrant inclusion of the name *Fort Stikine* on any list of the worst catastrophes that man has inflicted on himself.

The Kansu Earthquake – 1920

In some parts of China a curious legend holds sway. Under the earth, it is said, lives a dragon. And should that dragon wiggle its tail, a terrible shaking of the earth will ensue. On the bitterly cold night of December 16, 1920, the dragon gave its tail a mighty shake.

It was about 9:30 in the evening in China's Kansu Province, near the Tibetan border, when the people were awakened by a deafening roar. For a full half minute the earth pitched crazily one way, then the other. Hundreds of miles away at scientific stations, instruments recorded the intensity of the earthquake, which has since been rated as a violent 8.6 on the Richter scale, strong enough to carry the shocks over one and a half million square miles.

Throughout Kansu flimsy buildings tumbled to the ground. The earth groaned thunderously as it cracked into fissures large enough to swallow houses and camel trains. But the worst destruction was caused by the landslides that the earthquake touched off.

In much of Kansu Province, the soil is composed of loess, a dust-like mixture of clay and powdered quartz. There is little vegetation to anchor the slippery soil, and even in the best of times the people of Kansu had difficulty controlling the loess. Over the centuries they had developed an elaborate system of terraces to rein it in, but when the earthquake struck, terraces and natural formations alike collapsed, releasing the loess in a powdery avalanche so fluid that it cascaded through valleys as if it were water. In mountainside caves carved from the fragile earth thousands of sleeping peasants were buried alive as their dwellings disintegrated. Entire villages disappeared under the waves of loess.

In the light of day the next morning the few who had survived looked on a scene that bore little resemblance to what had been there just a day before. The terraced hillsides had collapsed. At least 10 cities and dozens of smaller settlements were shrouded in loess that had been made smooth by a raging wind, lending a surreal dimension to the devastation. The avalanche had dammed up rivers and transformed the region's valleys into muddy lakes. In short, the loess slides had created a whole new landscape, and some people say the Kansu earthquake changed the physical geography of the land like no other quake in modern history. The severity of the earthquake rates it as one of the world's worst ever.

The destruction radiated through an area of 15,000 square miles. More than 180,000 people were killed as a result of the earthquake and the subsequent landslide, and it was estimated that another 20,000 died from exposure in the months that followed, afraid to return to the caves and houses that had proven so inadequate in the face of the earthquake.

The disaster was so overwhelming, so unlike anything that part of China had previously experienced, that those who did survive coined a new phrase for what had happened on the night of December 16. *Shan tso-liao*, they called it: "The mountains walked."

OPPOSITE: *Two men and a horse are the only survivors in Sissiang, one of the towns destroyed by the December 1920 earthquake that struck China's Kansu Province. In the earthquake and aftermath, close to 200,000 people perished.*

RIGHT: *Missionaries amid the ruins of their headquarters at Liangehow, a town devastated by the 1920 earthquake.*

BELOW: *Kansu Province is included on a map indicating the location of some of world's worst earthquakes. The 1920 earthquake rates among the 20 most devastating quakes in history.*

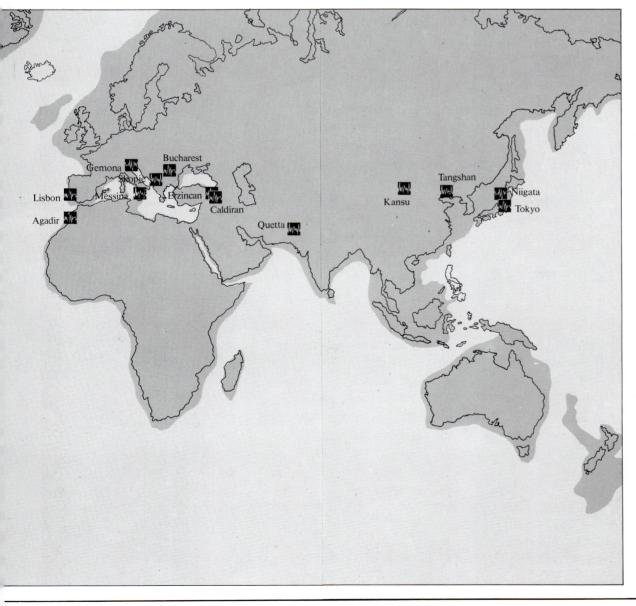

EARTHQUAKES: THE TOP TWENTY

Date	Place	Est. Deaths
1755	Lisbon, Portugal	6,000
1811	New Madrid, Missouri	Few known
1866	Peru and Ecuador	25,000
1906	San Francisco	500
1908	Messina, Italy	160,000
1920	Kansu, China	180,000
1923	Tokyo, Japan	143,000
1935	Quetta, Pakistan	60,000
1939	Erzincan, Turkey	40,000
1960	Agadir, Morocco	12,000
1963	Skopje, Yugoslavia	1,000
1964	Niigata, Japan	250
1964	Anchorage, Alaska	100
1971	Los Angeles	50
1972	Managua, Nicaragua	12,000
1975	Bucharest, Rumania	1,500
1976	Guatemala	23,000
1976	Gemona, Italy	1,000
1976	Caldiran, Turkey	8,000
1976	Tangshan, China	500,000

The Kanto Plain Earthquake – 1923

With 1500 earthquakes in their country every year, the Japanese greet most tremors with little more than a shrug. But the quake that struck the Kanto Plain, the heart of Japan's most populous area, at noon on September 1, 1923, was different. It started out no more impressively than any number of other earthquakes. Six minutes later, when the last tremor ceased, Japan had been shaken by one of the worst quakes in its history.

The earthquake-conscious Japanese were well-versed in what to do in case of a major quake: head for open spaces to avoid being crushed by falling buildings. As the gravity of the 1923 tremors became clear, people tumbled out into the streets of Tokyo and Yokohama and the other cities on the Kanto Plain. Numbers of the region's newer buildings had been constructed to withstand earthquakes. But these tremors were of such intensity – at some points the earth heaved 15 feet from side to side and dropped over six feet – that most of the new buildings simply collapsed. On top of this, the pitching of the earth set in motion a 36-foot tsunami that swamped Yokohama.

Then, as in San Francisco nearly two decades earlier, fire broke out. It had been lunchtime when the shocks began, and throughout Tokyo and Yokohama meals were being prepared on hibachis. When the quake struck the small stoves were hurled up against the paper walls of many homes, igniting them. Fanned by typhoon-force winds that had been blowing that morning, fires began spreading through the cities. There was almost no place to which people could escape.

Thousands who had initially raced for the streets were burned by fires that raged in the debris of fallen buildings. A huge mass of people (some estimates say as many as 24,000) huddled together in a park in Yokohama before being consumed by flames; they were so tightly packed, it was said, that many died standing up. Another 40,000 who took refuge at a military depot near Tokyo suffered a similar fate when a sudden gust of wind sent flames whirling into their midst. Thousands more who had dived into the Tokyo harbor for safety had just as horrendous a

ABOVE: *Fires touched off by the massive 1923 earthquake sweep through Tokyo, trapping thousands of people and destroying buildings. Striking Japan's heavily populated Kanto Plain, the earthquake claimed at least 143,000 lives.*

ABOVE RIGHT: *Designed by Frank Lloyd Wright, the Imperial Hotel was constructed with a steel framework that allowed it to "float" on its foundation. This photo, taken years later, shows the hotel that was one of Tokyo's few buildings left standing after the earthquake.*

RIGHT: *Japanese refugees and their salvaged belongings throng outside Tokyo's palace grounds, seeking an open place of safety, September 2, 1923.*

fate. Oil tanks there exploded, spreading fiery oil over the water and burning people alive.

The earthquake measured 8.3 on the Richter scale, and it was no surprise that most buildings fell in its wake. A few, however, withstood the assault, including architect Frank Lloyd Wright's new Imperial Hotel in Tokyo. Wright's design had not set well with some Japanese architects, who thought buildings needed a more stable base. Wright had chosen to construct his hotel with a steel framework that allowed it to "float" on top of the shaking ground.

The fact that Wright's building remained standing may have been architecturally significant, but it was little comfort to residents of Tokyo, Yokohama and the rest of the Kanto Plain. The death toll was enormous, with conservative estimates placing it at 143,000. Another 200,000 were injured. It was the three-day fire that followed the earthquake that was responsible for a great majority of the casualties.

Those who survived had nowhere to go. More than 600,000 buildings had been destroyed, leaving at least half a million people homeless. A 300-mile stretch that included Japan's two greatest cities now lay in ruins.

The Midwest Tornadoes – 1925

Tornadoes are a largely American phenomenon, seldom seen in any other country in the world. They are most apt to spring into being on the flat, open spaces of the Great Plains and Midwest states where weather systems come together without benefit of mountainous buffer zones. With its long finger-like funnel of air, a tornado can carve out a narrow and selective path, and it is not uncommon for one spot to be totally demolished while another, just a short distance away, is untouched.

People who hear that a twister is on the way brace for the worst. The sound is terrifying, like some gargantuan train bearing down. The sight is also terrifying, a dark funnel of wind jabbing viciously downward. And certainly the consequences can be terrifying. A person in the direct path of a twister has little chance of escape.

Perhaps the most destructive tornado system to strike the United States raced through the Ohio River Valley on March 18, 1925. There were at least eight separate tornadoes early on that spring afternoon, and they arrived with their customary lack of warning. One moment a railroad worker in the valley was gazing out the window and musing to a co-worker, "Guess it's gonna storm." The next minute he was picked up and tossed from the building.

The tornado system started out in eastern Missouri and darted and danced its way into Illinois, leveling some spots along the way and passing over others. For some of the time the twisters fanned out over a broad area; in other spots they merged and traveled as one. When the tornadoes did touch down, they were killers.

Only three people out of a population of 500 escaped injury in one town along the twister's path, and just one house was left standing. In West Frankfort, Illinois, the bodies of some victims were carried a mile and a half by the force of the wind. In nearby DeSoto the tornado smashed into a school dead-on. A trainman who saw what happened said there was "a crash of thunder preceded by two blinding flashes of lightning, after which there was nothing left." The building collapsed and caught fire, killing most of the children within. Afterwards, 25 small bodies were found where the playground had been.

The tornado continued its deadly game of tag all the way to Indiana, finally petering out as it approached Indianapolis. It was over in less than five hours. But in its wake it left at least 689 people dead in Missouri, Illinois and Indiana, and another 100 dead in neighboring states. Some 13,000 were injured and property damage reached $500 million.

The thousands of sightseers who drove down from the Chicago area in the days following the tornadoes saw bizarre tableaux: trains tossed about like toys; a barber's chair sitting upright in an open field; sheets and dresses clinging to fences and trees; a railroad bridge lifted off its supports. In one spot 40 automobiles had been piled together into a giant junkheap.

In 1974 an even broader span of the United States was ripped apart by a tornado outbreak with a range that dwarfed all tornadoes that had come before it. An astonishing 148 tornadoes raced across 2500 miles. But devastating as the 1974 tornadoes were, they still were not on the same scale as the 1925 twisters. In 1974 some 350 people died. That was less than half the number claimed a little less than 50 years earlier in the deadliest day of tornadoes the United States has ever seen.

ABOVE LEFT: *Part of the intense tornado system that wreaked havoc across the Midwest on March 18, 1925, this twister makes its way through western Indiana.*

LEFT: *Inhabitants of Xenia, Ohio, survey the damage after a tornado ripped through their town on April 3, 1974.*

ABOVE: *Survivors search through the wreckage of Griffen, Indiana, after the 1925 tornado.*

RIGHT: *This house in Xenia, Ohio, lost an entire wall to the '74 tornado.*

The Collapse of the St. Francis Dam – 1928

The St. Francis Dam in California was "fail-safe," a marvel of the latest engineering techniques when it was built in 1926. Its capacity was so enormous that it was said that the dam could supply Los Angeles, 40 miles to the south, with a full year's worth of water in an emergency.

The emergency, however, was to strike much closer to home. Early in the morning of March 13, 1928, the fail-safe dam failed.

The day before, a maintenance man had noticed a leak and notified the dam's designer, engineer William Mulholland. Leaks and cracks weren't uncommon in new dams, and Mulholland inspected the site and decided that the leak posed no immediate threat. Only 12 hours later two sides of the dam gave way, releasing 12 billion gallons of water into the canyon below.

The break was so sudden that there was no time to warn people asleep in their homes or in camps in the valley. Hundreds of houses belonging to ranchers and farmers were violently uprooted and washed along by a wave of water that reached nearly 100 feet high. A 3000-ton chunk of the concrete dam was found the next day over half a mile down the valley. Huge pieces of the dam smashed buildings to bits, and 600 homes were destroyed by the flood.

Some victims were found still in their nightclothes; others were partially dressed, perhaps getting ready to run for their lives. Eighty men housed in tents at a construction camp in the water's path were drowned. Some people managed to survive by clinging to pieces of debris and riding out the flood, but hundreds drowned or were buried in up to 30 feet of mud. On Highway 26 in the Santa Clara Valley 50 cars were washed from the road. Some, with their passengers still inside, were discovered days later buried in mud 20 miles from the highway.

Three hours after the dam broke the torrent had slowed to a trickle as its head reached the Pacific. But the valley lay strewn with bodies and debris, and rescuers were hampered by the thick layer of mud that was everywhere. Soon vultures were circling overhead. In all, at least 450 people died because of the collapse of the St. Francis Dam. Some estimates put the number as high as 700.

Immediately after the break there were rumors that an earthquake had cracked the dam open. But the real reason emerged soon enough. Mulholland, who had designed the St. Francis Dam as part of the aqueduct system that provided water to the Los Angeles area, was an engineer, not a geologist. But a project of this nature demanded the expertise of both. Mulholland's engineering was not faulted. Instead, officials blamed him for failing even to consult with geologists about the dam. The St. Francis was quite literally on shaky ground: gravelly rock on one side, weak layered rock on the other, and in the middle, powdery rock that dissolved when it came in contact with water. Given that fragile foundation, it was little wonder that the St. Francis Dam collapsed.

The work Mulholland had done in creating Los Angeles' vast aqueduct system had made him a legend in Southern California; the dam disaster proved that he was all too human. At an inquest the jury pointed out the obvious: "The construction and operation of a great dam should never be left to the sole judgment of one man, no matter how eminent." Mulholland shouldered the blame manfully. "Don't blame anyone else," he said. "You just fasten it on me. If there was an error of human judgment, I was the human."

LEFT: *A view of California's San Francisquito Canyon after the collapse of the St. Francis dam in 1928. The water in the valley is receding, leaving behind a thick layer of mud.*

ABOVE: *This house in the flood's path was carried for many feet by the force of the rushing waters after the disastrous dam collapse, which claimed at least 450 lives.*

The Yellow River Flood – 1931

Of all the world's great rivers, it is China's Yellow River that is by far the most flood-prone, and over the past 40 centuries it has claimed millions of lives. It is little wonder, then, that in China the Yellow is known by another name: "The Sorrow."

It was along the Yellow River that Chinese civilization was born some 7000 years ago. The plain surrounding the river is composed almost entirely of silt and is perhaps the most fertile land in the world. Fully one-fifth of China's farmland is in the North China Plain, the home of the Yellow. But the region's shaky foundation of silt makes man's use of the land a risky venture. A visitor to the North China Plain around the turn of this century observed that there "Man belongs to the soil, not the soil to man."

In the past 3500 years the Yellow has flooded 1500 times. This, despite the perennial labors of the Chinese to tame the river with an elaborate system of dikes that in some spots channeled it into an elevated path 30 feet high. It is the Yellow River's peculiar relation with the land that has made it so prone to flooding. Farther south in China, the Yangtze River carries more water than the Yellow, but the Yangtze travels through channels and gorges that can usually contain at least some of the high water after rains. The Yellow has no such help from the land: when rains occur there are no hills and mountains to prevent the water from going where it will. It simply spreads like a puddle on a smooth floor.

The silt in the Yellow River, which gives it its name, has added to the problems. Instead of collecting along the water's edge and forming a bank, the fine silt in the Yellow falls evenly along the river bed, eliminating any deep channels that could hold the water in check.

In 1887 a catastrophic flood – even for the Yellow –

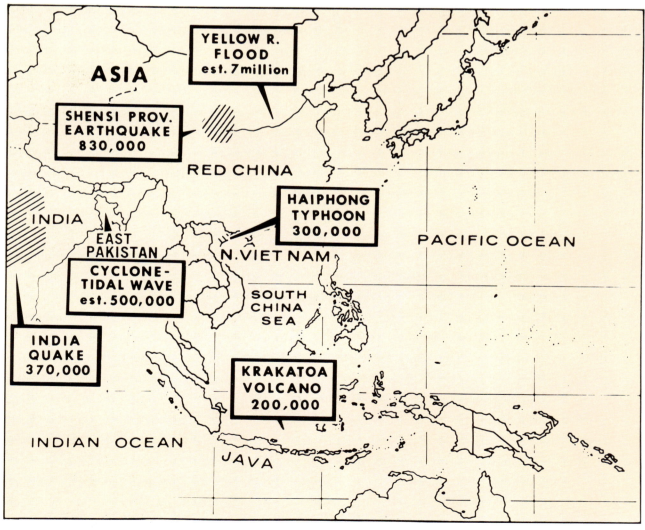

killed an estimated 900,000 people. It was called the worst flood in human history, but nearly half a century later, in August of 1931, another flood that was even more devastating swamped the Yellow River. This time the loss of life was so enormous as to be almost incomprehensible. Some sources reported that 3.7 million people died as a result of the 1931 flood, a number roughly equal to the present population of Los Angeles. And in 1938 another flood and famine battered the region yet again.

Soon after it came to power in 1949 the People's Republic of China embarked on a 50-year plan to bring the river under control with dams, basins and traditional dikes. Since then nearly half a million workers have descended on the region every dry season to try to tame the Yellow, spurred on by the words of Mao Tse-Tung: "Work on the Yellow River must be done well!" Time will tell if the Chinese succeed — or if the Yellow River's history continues to repeat itself.

LEFT: *An aerial view of villages along China's Yellow River, swamped by the cataclysmic flood of August 1931. Note the broken and overflowed dikes along the riverbank.*

BELOW, FAR LEFT: *A map of some of the worst disasters to befall Southeast Asia includes the 1887 flooding of the Yellow River, which* killed 900,000 people in Honan Province alone.

BELOW: *Floodwaters during the 1931 Chinese calamity approach the rooftops, as refugees make their way along elevated railroad tracks. The flood of '31 was estimated by some sources to have caused 3.7 million deaths.*

The Ohio River Floods – 1937

The industrial cities along the Ohio River were just emerging from the Depression as 1937 began. Factories were back in operation, rail lines were busy and workers were feeling better about what the future held. Then that sunny picture was upset by something that had nothing to do with manufacturing orders or interest rates. It started to rain.

January is often a rainy month along the Ohio Valley. But in January of 1937 it truly rained. And rained. And all the while the clouds hovered almost directly above the Ohio, not spreading far enough for tributaries to accommodate any of the water. By January 18 a long stretch of the Ohio had flooded, and water was rushing down on to the Mississippi as well. Two days later the river rose over six feet. By January 24, which came to be known as Black Sunday, the entire Ohio was at flood stage and water was raging out of control. In Evansville, Indiana, 400 blocks of the city were submerged.

Weather watchers were astounded by the amount of precipitation. One estimate said that 165 billion tons of rain fell in that single month, enough to put eight million acres under water.

This wasn't the first time the Ohio and Mississippi Rivers had had flooding problems, however, and in the years prior to 1937 much thought had been devoted to how to deal with the next bad flood. The Flood Control Act of 1928 had provided for a system of levees and reservoirs to handle at least some of the overflow. The 1937 flood would test just how well the plan worked.

At Cairo, Illinois, where the Ohio and the Mississippi meet, the water had risen to over 55 feet by the end of January. Fearful for the city, the Army Corps of Engineers dynamited a levee to divert some of the Mississippi's water into a floodway, and the threat to Cairo was averted. Down in New Orleans, the rush of water coursing down the Mississippi was channeled into Lake Pontchartrain. But many of the tributaries along the Ohio and Mississippi Rivers didn't have these back-ups available to handle the extra water. Wholesale flooding was inevitable, and flood it did, as one community after another was swamped.

By the end of January, one and a half million people in a 12-state area were in need of help. The American Red Cross, bolstered by an outpouring of donations from throughout the United States, stepped in to oversee the relief efforts. In more than 1500 tent cities and 300 makeshift hospitals scattered across the river valley the Red Cross cared for nearly 700,000 people. A flotilla of 7000 boats was assembled in just five days to transport people and supplies to the camps.

Even with the Red Cross' help, conditions were grim. Water sources had been contaminated, and supplies of drinking water were strictly rationed. There was fear of a typhoid epidemic, and a campaign to inoculate flood victims began. Thousands of bewildered youngsters were housed at the camps but even the games and toys provided by the Junior Red Cross didn't change the fact that many had been separated from their families.

Some 250 deaths were directly attributable to the flood, and nearly 1000 more people may have died from illness or injuries related to it. Thirteen thousand homes were gone, and property damage amounted to $300 million, making the flood of 1937 one of the worst in United States history.

OPPOSITE TOP: *Plantation workers and convicts labor to strengthen the levee along the Mississippi River at South Memphis, Tennessee, on January 31, 1937.*

OPPOSITE CENTER: *Evacuation proceedings begin at Cairo, Illinois, on January 28.*

LEFT: *Refugees take advantage of a temporary pontoon bridge in Louisville, Kentucky.*

ABOVE: *Lawrenceberg, Indiana, is almost completely submerged.*

RIGHT: *Few floods in American history rival the legendary Johnstown, Pennsylvania, flood of May 31, 1889.*

The Explosion of the *Hindenburg* – 1937

The actual death toll was small. When the German zeppelin *Hindenburg* exploded in flames early on the evening of May 6, 1937, just 36 passengers and crew died. But the end of the *Hindenburg* was such spectacle that it instantly earned a reputation as one of history's great disasters.

The *Hindenburg* was the pride of the German airship fleet, the largest such craft ever built. It was kept aloft by hydrogen (most airships in the United States had switched to helium, which was not flammable) and traveled at speeds of up to 84 miles per hour. The *Hindenburg's* 8000-mile range, passenger-carrying capacity and ability to fly through certain types of bad weather gave it a distinct advantage over airplanes of the day. Nearly 100 passengers could travel in luxurious comfort in 25 staterooms and gather in a cocktail lounge fitted with a grand piano made of lightweight aluminum. In its first year, 1936, the *Hindenburg* made 10 transatlantic crossings and seemed to merit the claim that it was the world's greatest airship.

The *Hindenburg* was completing its first Atlantic crossing of 1937 as it approached the Lakehurst, New Jersey, Naval Air Station on the afternoon of May 6. Bad weather rolled into the area, however, and the landing was delayed until word came that conditions had improved. Over a thousand spectators were on hand to watch as the huge silvery ship came into view at about 7 PM.

The *Hindenburg* descended to less than 200 feet and dropped its landing lines to the waiting ground crew. But

ABOVE: *The* Hindenburg *is secured at Frankfurt am Main, Germany, after an early record-breaking 48-hour flight. The much-heralded airship made 10 transatlantic crossings in 1936 before its ill-fated crossing in 1937.*

LEFT: *After exploding, the burning* Hindenburg *slowly sinks to the ground at the Naval Air Station at Lakehurst, New Jersey, on May 6, 1937. Out of 97 passengers and crew on board, 35 were killed; many were able to leap out the windows to safety.*

FAR RIGHT, ABOVE: *The enormous skeleton of the* Hindenburg *smolders after its tragic demise.*

RIGHT: *The New York* Times *featured the* Hindenburg *disaster on the front page of its May 7 edition, relaying to an astonished nation all that was known at the time.*

The New York Times.

HINDENBURG BURNS IN LAKEHURST CRASH;
21 KNOWN DEAD, 12 MISSING; 64 ESCAPE

THE HINDENBURG IN FLAMES ON THE FIELD AT LAKEHURST
The giant airliner as she settled to the ground near her mooring mast at 7:23 o'clock last night.

the ship had too much momentum and floated past the mooring mast. As the crew adjusted the ballast and ropes, the *Hindenburg*'s nose dipped gently, then rose as the tail sank. Suddenly there was a flash of light, and the *Hindenburg* burst into flames.

It was a moment before the passengers who had been leaning out of the gondola windows to watch the landing realized that the *Hindenburg* had exploded. Consumed by fire, the airship sank as if in slow motion to the ground. Some passengers leaped from the windows when the ship was still far above the landing area; others slid down the landing ropes to safety. Sailors from the air stations scrambled forward to pull people from the wreck, and a few in the bow section were able to walk away unassisted. But out of 97 passengers and crew on board, 35 were killed, along with one member of the ground crew. Shortly after the giant airframe touched down it was nothing more than a skeleton of girders and struts.

The cause of the *Hindenburg* crash was steeped in intrigue from the moment it happened. Some laid the blame on the electrical storm that had delayed the airship's landing, saying that a spark from the charged air somehow ignited the seven million cubic feet of hydrogen that kept the ship airborne. The risks of hydrogen were well-documented: fully half of the nearly 150 airships that had used the gas had experienced fires. Others sketched out a more sinister scenario, contending that the *Hindenburg*, Adolf Hitler's symbol of German technological superiority, was sabotaged by the country's enemies.

Whatever the cause, the demise of the *Hindenburg* was more than the loss of a single craft. The first commercial airship to explode, the *Hindenburg*'s passing marked the end of an era. In the space of a few minutes, commercial aviation had changed forever, and "lighter-than-air ships" were a thing of the past.

The New England Hurricane – 1938

New England has never been considered hurricane country; in the United States that dubious distinction has belonged to areas farther south along the Atlantic coast and the Gulf of Mexico. But in September 1938 the "Great New England Hurricane," as it would come to be known, would strike with such force that all future New England storms would be measured against it.

The hurricane began slowly off the coast of Africa in the first few days of September. From there it made its way across the Atlantic and threatened Florida before backing off and moving north parallel to the coastline, but not touching it. The news media made little of the offshore storm; in those pre-World War II days, they were more concerned with what was going on in Europe. Ironically, preoccupation with events 3000 miles away opened the door for a disaster at home.

On September 21 the morning weather forecasts in the Northeast were merely warning of a low pressure system. It was "business as usual" for most people. But by the afternoon, the area was in the grips of a full-fledged hurricane – and was grossly unprepared for it.

New York City was the first to be hit. The Empire State Building, then the world's tallest structure, began swaying as much as four inches in the 120 miles per hour winds. Subways in the city were flooded. On Long Island the hurricane leveled beach communities, including 153 of the 179 houses in the wealthy town of Westhampton. The social club there, the scene of parties just weeks before, became a makeshift morgue for the bodies of those killed by the winds and the waves.

Racing along at over 50 miles per hour, the hurricane pounded up the coast. Gusts of over 180 miles per hour were recorded at several spots along its path. In New Haven, Connecticut, an entire amusement park slid into the ocean. In Providence, Rhode Island, at the head of the Narragansett Bay, streets were flooded 12 feet deep. The roof blew off the city's train station, and people who tried to climb to the tops of railroad cars for safety were washed away. Guests in the lobby of one Rhode Island hotel drowned when waves poured in upon them.

In Springfield, Massachusetts, 16,000 shade trees fell. Vermont sugar maple stands were cut down by the hurricane, as were acres of apple orchards. Crops were lost, poultry flocks decimated.

By the time the storm made its way through Massachusetts and Vermont and then petered out in Canada, it was on the way to establishing itself as perhaps the worst hurricane ever to strike the Northeast. More than 500 people were killed in the storm and another 100 never accounted for. Nearly 2000 more were injured. There were estimates that 93,000 were left homeless. Property damage was staggering, eventually coming to well over $300 million. Fourteen thousand buildings were destroyed, 25,000 boats were sunk and three-quarters of a million farm animals were lost.

In years to come the same part of the country would be hit by more fierce storms: Hurricane Carol in 1954, Diane in 1955. Both storms would cause property losses, but thanks to advanced weather forecasting warning systems, loss of life would be far below that caused by the 1938 storm. To people in the Northeast, it remains the "Great New England Hurricane."

ABOVE LEFT: *An aerial view of an estate in Westhampton, Long Island, destroyed by the violent hurricane of 1938. Winds and water leveled many of Long Island's beach communities, including this wealthy town.*

ABOVE: *Downtown Providence, Rhode Island, is swamped after being struck by Hurricane Carol on September 2, 1954. One of the cities hardest hit by the hurricane of 1938, Providence suffered much damage from this raging storm 16 years later.*

RIGHT: *Crazily tilted telephone poles on Rockaway, Long Island, testify to the strength of the 1938 hurricane's 120-miles per hour winds.*

LEFT: *In New London, Connecticut, boats were hurled together and the waterfront ravaged by the fierce 1938 hurricane. By the time the storm had made its way through New England, more than 500 people were killed.*

BELOW: *The torrential rains and ravaging winds of the 1938 hurricane turned the quiet streets of Winchester, Massachusetts, into raging torrents as nearby rivers overflowed their banks.*

RIGHT: *The historic steeple of Old North Church – from which lanterns hung to warn of a British attack in 1775 – lies shattered on the ground after Hurricane Carol swept through Boston on September 1, 1954.*

BELOW: *In the aftermath of Hurricane Diane, which hit the Northeast on August 8, 1955, a house in East Stroudsburg, Pennsylvania, lies in ruins. The hurricane caused $458 million in property damage, and left 179 people dead.*

BOTTOM: *Typical of many coastline streets of New York and New Jersey after Hurricane Carol ravaged the Northeast in 1954, this flooded street in Babylon, Long Island, is blocked by a fallen tree and littered with disabled vehicles.*

The Cocoanut Grove Fire – 1942

Business was booming at Boston's Cocoanut night-club in the early 1940s; the stresses of war had left people looking for places to forget their worries. On the night of November 28, 1942, however, the club was especially crowded, even by wartime standards. Holy Cross had just upset Boston College in a football game, and hundreds of people had headed straight from the field to the Cocoanut Grove to celebrate or commiserate. On top of that, it was Thanksgiving weekend, and soldiers and sailors were living it up at the end of their holiday leaves. Over a thousand people – more than twice the legal capacity – had jammed into the club that night.

The decorators of the Cocoanut Grove had worked hard to create the illusion of a tropical paradise, and the club was decked out with artificial palm trees, leather walls and ceilings of sky-blue satin. It was all very colorful and exotic. And highly flammable.

A little before 10:00 a patron in the downstairs room of the club decided to improve upon the atmosphere. He reached up to unscrew a lightbulb; a busboy noticed and hurried over to replace the bulb. The busboy balanced on a chair and lit a match to see what he was doing. The match burned his fingers, he dropped in into a palm tree and in moments the festive mood in the Cocoanut Grove was a thing of the past.

The artificial tree burst into flames that quickly traveled across the ceiling. A woman's panic-stricken voice cried "Fire!" and suddenly the patrons were in a frenzy, knocking down chairs and climbing over tables as they rushed up the stairs to a door that led outside.

The door was locked. As couples upstairs continued to socialize and dance, oblivious to the screams and crashing of glass from below, the crowd from the basement lounge now headed for the revolving door at the club's main entrance. That door, too, failed, jammed shut by the mob of people pushing into it. By now the fire was intense, and dozens of people were trapped in the doorways.

In minutes the flames had raced up the stairs and reached the Cocoanut Grove's main dining room. Thick smoke was billowing through the club, produced, ironically, by a fire-resistant chemical that had been sprayed on the leather walls. Half-blinded, people fumbled toward the exits, only to find that almost every one of the doors was locked. Soon the exits would be blocked by the bodies of those who had struggled to escape and failed.

Only half of the patrons of the Cocoanut Grove that night managed to get out. Some crawled through basement windows in their evening clothes; others made their way upstairs and jumped from windows. When the final body count was completed 491 people had lost their lives in the Cocoanut Grove fire.

They were victims, for the most part, of panic and the club's poor design. The building's main revolving door had broken in the crush of frenzied people streaming into it. The majority of the club's other doors had been locked. Those that were functional opened in, not out, restricting the passage of people to the outside.

Firefighters attempting to enter the building were stymied by the piles of bodies in front of the doors. When they finally could enter, they discovered that most of the victims had died from smoke inhalation, not burns. Others had been trampled to death in the desperate crush of people looking for a way out. Boston's building commissioner said, "It was evident that a terrific fight had taken place in the darkness and tumult of the panic."

The Boston College football team had planned to celebrate that night at the Cocoanut Grove, but after their humiliating loss to Holy Cross they felt in no mood for revelry and decided to stay home. It was a decision they never regretted.

LEFT: *Firemen survey the charred ruins of Boston's Cocoanut Grove night club the day after the lethal blaze caused 491 deaths. Half of the patrons escaped through windows.*

ABOVE RIGHT: *Two days after the Cocoanut Grove fire, cars remain in a parking lot at the rear of the night club. Driven to the club by fire victims, these cars were never claimed by their original owners.*

RIGHT: *Firemen stand in what remains of the revolving door behind the burnt-out facade of the Cocoanut Grove night club after the deadly fire of November 28, 1942.*

Death on the Black Market Express – 1944

It was supposed to be just a freight run, but the *Balvano Limited*, which traveled between Naples and Lucania, Italy, during World War II, was commonly known as the "Black Market Express." Each week hundreds of men would hide themselves illegally in the train's empty freight cars, then head for the countryside to pick up meat, produce and other hard-to-get items that they could sell at a wartime premium in occupied Naples. Early in March of 1944 these stowaways became victims of one of the worst railroad disasters in history.

Only six crew members, plus a group of medical students just finished with a training exercise, should have been on board the train, but several hundred more had found places in one of the 42 cars and had settled in for the ride into the Italian hill country. Usually two engines were enough to pull the train along easily. But on this run the presence of the students and stowaways probably put the train as much as 11 tons over its customary weight. As the *Balvano Limited* started its climb into the mountains the extra load and icy tracks began to take their toll. But despite the reduced pace, the crew continued to stoke the engines with low-grade wartime coal, and the train managed to stagger along its route.

BOTTOM: *Italian officials relieve the "Black Market Express" of its ghastly load after the train stalled in the Galleria delle Armi tunnel on its way east from Naples on March 8, 1944.*

BELOW: *A terse report of the disaster appeared in an Irish edition of the U.S. Army newspaper,* Stars and Stripes.

RIGHT: *A truck filled with bodies from the* Balvano Limited *disaster arrives at the mortuary. Over 500 passengers were asphyxiated when the tunnel filled with poisonous carbon monoxide.*

500 Italians Die As Train Breaks Down In Tunnel

NAPLES, March 8 (Reuter)—More than 500 Italians died—most of them from asphyxiation—when a train broke down in a railroad tunnel in central-southern Italy Friday. The weight of hundreds of Italians who swarmed on the train as it traveled eastward disabled the engine. Engine fumes caused a majority of the deaths.

50

The *Limited* stopped for just over half an hour in a tunnel while it waited for another train to clear the tracks, then resumed its plodding trek upwards toward the long Galleria delle Armi tunnel. From this point on, no one is quite sure just what happened.

The train was by now clearly in difficulty. Its weight, the steep grade and the treacherous ice on the tracks were all working against it, and once in the tunnel the *Balvano Limited* ground to a halt, then slipped backwards. Straining to pull their load forward, the engines belched thick clouds of smoke into the tunnel.

Minutes, then hours, passed. In the caboose, which had been pushed out of the tunnel when the train slipped backwards, the brakeman began to wonder what was wrong. He was accustomed to delays, but this was much longer than usual. He climbed down from the caboose and began to make his way along the tunnel. Almost immediately he knew why the train had come to a dead halt.

Poisonous carbon monoxide gas produced by the cheap wartime coal had filled the tunnel, trapped there with no place to go. Now, in every car, groups of men lay sprawled as if asleep. In fact, they were dead.

The brakeman sped on foot for help. Meanwhile, the stationmaster at the nearest depot was growing concerned and sent an engine up the tracks to find out what was delaying the *Balvano Limited*. When the engine arrived it came upon an eerie scene. The crewmen in the engine cars were dead, along with the hundreds of passengers in the freight cars. "The faces of the victims were mostly peaceful," a rescuer recalled. "They showed no sign of suffering. Many were sitting upright or in positions they might assume while sleeping normally."

Because it was wartime the Allied government censored most of the details of the accident; a tiny item about it was buried on the inside pages of *The New York Times*. Two weeks later the government's investigation of the accident was released. A stalled train, slippery rails and weather conditions had combined to asphyxiate the passengers on the *Balvano Limited* in what investigators called "an act of God." The report said that 426 people had died. When details of the accident finally emerged after the war the figure would swell to over 500.

The Hilo Tsunami – 1946

In the early morning hours of April 1, 1946, 70 miles off the Alaskan coast, a violent earthquake was taking place deep under the sea, making it seem as if the bottom had fallen from the ocean floor. Into the gap rushed tons of water, setting in motion a steadily growing series of waves.

Within minutes the earthquake had sent a 100-foot wave crashing over a nearby Alaskan lighthouse. But that was only the beginning. From Alaska the waves would travel 8000 miles, bouncing off the coast of California then smashing up against Chile. It was in the middle of their arcing path through the Pacific, however, that they would produce their most dramatic effect. Five hours after the earthquake occurred, and 2000 miles away from its center, a killer tsunami would virtually wipe out the town of Hilo on Hawaii's unprotected northeast coast.

In the meantime, the tsunami made its way stealthily across the Pacific. Its waves were modest, just two feet high, so it traveled along the open ocean undetected. But though the waves may have been small, they were propelled by a force great enough to send them racing along at speeds of over 450 miles per hour. When the waves reached the shallow waters off the coast of Hawaii the tsunami's power suddenly became clear. It crested and stormed over the beach at Hilo: three waves, three minutes apart, reaching heights of 50 feet.

The island hardly knew what had hit it. Before the waves arrived on shore only a hissing sound that grew steadily louder had offered a clue as to what was in store for Hilo.

The huge wall of water knocked beach houses apart and dragged dozens of beach dwellers out to sea. People climbed palm trees to escape the surging water or ran on foot for high ground. Cars, trains, trucks and boats were tossed about like toys. After the wave receded, rescue workers set about digging out the victims who had been trapped in wreckage or buried in the silt – up to 14 feet of it – deposited by the wave.

The 1946 tsunami was the 37th to strike the Hawaiian Islands over the course of the past century. But it was by far the most destructive. The death toll throughout the island chain reached 173; 163 more were injured. Over a thousand buildings were destroyed, and property damages totalled $25 million.

The tsunami delivered a clear message: lack of warning had proved fatal, and Hawaii urgently needed a way to alert its people to an approaching tsunami. Prompted to act by the large losses of April 1, the U.S. Coast and Geodetic Survey set to work on the task that same day.

The Seismic Wave Warning System that resulted was tested in May of 1960 when another tsunami was bearing down on Hilo. Sirens were sounded throughout the city and residents were urged to evacuate. But not everyone who heard the warnings heeded them. Only a third of the people aware that a tsunami was on its way chose to leave the area, and some were foolhardy enough to head down to the sea, instead of away from it, to watch the waves bear down on them. Despite a carefully orchestrated emergency plan, the 1960 tsunami still managed to take 61 lives.

OPPOSITE: *An aerial view of Hilo's waterfront four days after the devastating tsunami of April 1, 1946. The series of three 50-foot tidal waves smashed the Hawaiian community with such force that those in its path had little chance of escape.*

RIGHT: *Main Street in Hilo is piled high with the buildings demolished by the tsunami.*

BELOW: *Fishing boats perch on a pier at Japan's Hachinohe Harbor on Honshu after being washed ashore by tidal waves caused by the Chilean earthquake of May 26, 1960. A tsunami caused by that same earthquake also hit Hilo, but a warning system allowed some time for evacuation.*

The London Killer Smog – 1952

For centuries writers and artists have depicted "Foggy London Town" as a city cloaked in a romantic mist. But that cliché lost its charm in December, 1952, when the fog turned deadly.

Thursday, December 4, dawned chilly and gray — nothing new for Londoners. The weather was about to take a peculiar turn, however. As the day went on a high pressure system moved over southern England. The wind died down, and over the Thames River the early morning cold was trapped under a suffocating blanket of warm air. By evening a heavy fog had begun to form.

Londoners, chilled by the cold air trapped near the ground, were busily stoking up their coal fires. Factories routinely spewed their daily doses of sulfurous smoke into the air. There was no wind to blow the heavy smoke away, and the same weather system that had trapped the cold air near the ground and sent Londoners indoors to huddle around their hearths now worked to trap smoke from the chimneys close to the ground. By Friday, a freezing day with high humidity and no wind, a dense smog was forming over the city.

Saturday and Sunday brought more of the same. Factories and homes continued to send out smoke. The sky took on a yellowish cast, then brown. By the weekend's close, the air was nearly coal-black.

Traffic came to a standstill because drivers could not make out the road before them. Cars were abandoned, deliveries halted. People on the streets, blinded by the smog, could barely recognize objects only a few feet in front of them; some wandered onto the railroad tracks or into the river and died. On December 9 a strong wind moved in and swept the smog away. But, in fact, London was only now going to see its true effects.

Hospitals were jammed with patients suffering from severe breathing difficulties: hacking coughs, shortness of breath. People with respiratory ailments were hit hard, and the weakest — the very young and the very old — became seriously ill. Then, in the space of days, patients started dying. As deaths rose into the hundreds, then thousands, doctors realized that this particular smog had been more deadly than an air raid.

There were long lines of people waiting to register their relatives' deaths. The city morgues ran out of shrouds. The wait for burial in some London cemeteries reached 10 days. Estimates of the dead ranged from 4000 to as high as 8000, and smog-related deaths continued to be reported into January. Said one Member of Parliament, "It's almost on the scale of a mass extermination."

The killing smog spurred newspapers and Parliament to demand action, and the result was a Clean Air Act giving local governments the power to declare fog emergencies. In 1962 a fog almost identical to the one of 1952 covered London. But the government now had the authority to shut down polluting factories, and the difference it made was clear. The death toll exacted by the 1962 fog was a fraction of what it had been 10 years earlier.

LEFT: *Wearing a smog mask to filter toxins out of the air, a young woman chats with a London cabbie at midday — although the fog is so dense it seems like night time. The combination of weather factors and pollutants caused such a deadly smog to form over London in December, 1952, that smog-related deaths climbed into the thousands.*

RIGHT: *The killing London smog lasted five days, and when it was over disbelief at the casualty count soon turned to outrage. Public pressure brought about the formation of a Clean Air Act.*

The Holland Floods – 1953

There's an old saying that goes, "God created the world, except Holland; *it* was made by the Dutch." The people of The Netherlands know that their country sits on borrowed land, and over centuries they have built hundreds of dikes to protect it from a jealous sea. For much of that time, the dikes have held. In 1953, however, the sea would prove too strong.

Three forces of nature joined together in February of that year to swamp The Netherlands. There were the usual high tides of spring, but with the added pull of a full moon and sun in direct line with the earth, the tides ran even higher. And off to the west, a hurricane was brewing in the Atlantic and bearing down on the North Sea. On February 1 wind, rain and tides brought the water to levels that had not been seen since the great Dutch floods of the sixteenth century. Holland was once again under attack by the sea, but this time the country's elaborate system of dikes would not be equal to the task.

Such faith did the Dutch have in their bulwarks against the sea that they shrugged off the earliest signs that a major flood was in the offing. One woman who heard water splashing about in her daughter's kitchen concluded that she'd merely spilled the teakettle; another thought the sound of sloshing water in her house was due to finicky plumbing. The gravity of the situation soon became apparent, however. When 50 dikes broke almost simultaneously, more than 100 villages and towns were inundated.

The keepers of the dikes had tolled the traditional churchbell warnings when the barriers burst, but for many it was too late. In some spots the water rose 16 feet in just a quarter of an hour. People began scrambling for the second stories of their homes, then the attics, finally the roofs. For some even that wasn't high enough. One man was rescued after dangling from the crossbars of a telephone pole for more than two days. Another had escaped the flood waters by suspending himself from telephone wires.

Thousands of men and women, however, did what the Dutch have always done in times of flood: they headed for the dikes to pump water, wield shovels and carry sandbags. In one town 100 fishermen formed a human seawall to shore up the dikes; in another, a captain saw a break in the dike and rammed his ship into it like a giant cork. Men worked feverishly to fortify the dikes protecting the great Dutch cities of Amsterdam, Rotterdam and The Hague, where three million people lived. The water rose to unheard-of levels, but the workers' diligence paid off. These dikes held.

But even the most heroic acts could not prevent the water from overcoming hundreds. Nearly 2000 Dutch men, women and children died from the floods and the freezing cold that followed. England was also hard hit, with over 300 dead, and more fatalities were reported in Belgium.

Nearly one-tenth of the farmland in The Netherlands was under water, and half a million head of livestock were lost. Estimates of the property damage ranged from $300 to $500 million. In other parts of the world, people wondered why the Dutch did not simply give up on a place so vulnerable to flooding. In reply the government pointed to the example of centuries of Dutch tradition: "We do not abandon our land." Then they set to work to make sure it would not happen again.

ABOVE: *Rescued calves are taken off a boat in Gravendeel, Holland, in February, 1953. High tides and a hurricane produced the Netherlands' worst flood in centuries.*

BELOW: *England and Belgium were also hard hit by flooding in February of 1953. Here, Britain's Canvey Island is swamped by seawater that swept over the barrier.*

RIGHT: *On Holland's Shoowen Island, workers repair an ocean barrier.*

BELOW RIGHT: *In Zeebrugge, Belgium, flood waters drain into a collapsed culvert.*

Typhoon Vera – 1959

Most Pacific typhoons that approach Japan veer off before getting the chance to do much damage ashore. But by September of 1959 the country's luck was wearing thin. Japan had been hit by four typhoons already that year, and now weather forecasters warned of yet another on the way. This one, they cautioned, could be a "supertyphoon." On September 26 their prediction came true.

Typhoon Vera hit Honshu, Japan's most heavily settled island, with a vengeance. Winds of 92 miles per hour whipped through Tokyo and Yokohama, and Vera's rain flooded city streets and halted rail traffic. Seventeen-foot-high waves pounded Honshu's eastern coast before Vera changed course and attacked the island's northern provinces.

But it was Japan's third-largest city, Nagoya, that was to bear the brunt of the storm. Located south of Yokohama, Nagoya had a population of over a million and was an important industrial center for the nation. In 1959 the city was preparing to mark its 70th anniversary with parades and fireworks. Typhoon Vera put an end to any thoughts Nagoya had of celebrating in style.

The typhoon blasted the city with winds powerful enough to hurl a ship weighing more than 7000 tons onto the rocks of the city's harbor. Six more ocean-going vessels were also grounded, and 25 fishing boats sank. In the city itself the flooding wrecked nearly 6000 homes in minutes. That flimsy little buildings were falling everywhere was perhaps not altogether surprising, but Vera packed such force that even a firmly anchored apartment building toppled, pinning 84 people inside.

Winds of over 135 miles per hour drove the typhoon's rain down onto Nagoya, and in some spots the water rose so fast that people had to smash holes through their roofs to keep their heads above water. Those who could not reach safety fast enough were carried away. The water swirled through Nagoya's lumberyards, releasing thousands of logs that then swept through the city like battering rams, smashing through doors and shuttered windows.

Even after Vera had moved on, rescue efforts by helicopters sent in to pluck people from the roofs were made difficult by continued high wind and water. A week after the typhoon had spent herself the city of Nagoya was still reeling. Rescuers found 25,000 people stranded on rooftops, sustained only by bits of food gleaned from forays into the murky waters to retrieve a vegetable or two from the family garden. Hundreds of bodies drifted in the flood waters. Soon hunger was the new threat, along with disease from lack of sanitary water.

When the final reports were in on Typhoon Vera they were shocking. Some 5000 people were dead. Thousands more were missing, and over a million people were homeless. Japan's transportation was in tatters, with more than 800 breaks reported in the rail lines. Property damage totalled three-quarters of a billion dollars. Typhoon Vera had caused more destruction than any previous storm in modern Japanese history.

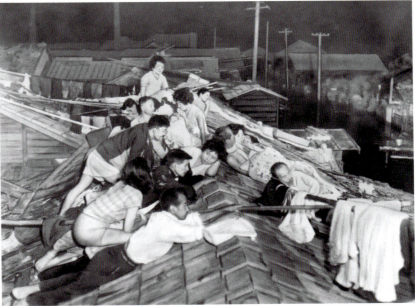

FAR LEFT: *Police and firemen search for survivors in the collapsed ruins of two apartment houses after Typhoon Vera demolished much of Nagoya, Japan, on September 26, 1959.*

LEFT: *The main street of Nagoya is strewn with debris in the aftermath of the catastrophic typhoon, which claimed at least 500 lives in Japan.*

TOP: *Crumpled pearl-farming rafts are washed ashore at Ago Bay, after Typhoon Vera swept an estimated 75 million pearl oysters, valued at over $10 million, away.*

ABOVE: *Survivors of Japan's worst typhoon spend the night on a rooftop in Nagoya. Thousands of Nagoya's inhabitants were stranded on roofs for a week before help could get to them.*

The Sinking of USS *Thresher* – 1963

In the tense atmosphere of the Cold War years the nuclear-powered USS *Thresher* was just the kind of new submarine the United States Navy needed. She could run more silently, deeper and faster than any sub that had come before.

But in stretching the limits of the new technology the *Thresher* had acquired a number of bugs that needed to be worked out of her system. The ship had spent two-thirds

LEFT: *Photographed in April, 1962, crewmen go about their business on the USS* Thresher, *the submarine that was lost – with 129 men aboard – on a test dive in 1963.*

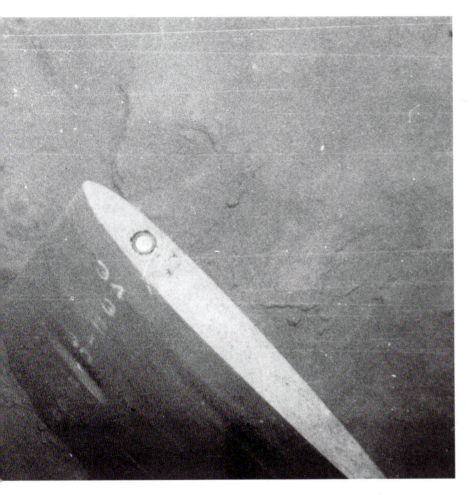

TOP: *This photo, obtained by the deep-diving bathyscaph* Trieste II, *is an overhead view of the dorsal rudder of the* Thresher, *lying on the ocean floor.*

ABOVE: *The sub rescue vessel* Skylark *remains at the site where the* Thresher *submerged for the last time, directing rescue vessels two days later.*

of the time since her launching in dry dock, where more than 850 defects were corrected.

By the spring of 1963, however, she was ready to be tested, and on April 9 the *Thresher* headed out of Portsmouth Naval Shipyard in New Hampshire for a series of routine shallow dives. The next day she was underway to the Wilkenson Deep in the North Atlantic to test her mettle in the deepest waters. On board was the standard crew of 112, plus 17 civilians there to observe the test.

As she dove deeper and deeper the *Thresher* reported her progress to the sub-rescue vessel that accompanied her, the *Skylark*. At the time of the first report, 7:52 AM, the *Thresher* was at 300 feet. Several more progress reports followed. At 9:12 the sub was at 1000 feet. Just a minute later a garbled but troubling message came through on the *Skylark's* radio: "Experiencing minor problem . . . have positive angle . . . attempting to blow." The *Skylark* asked for position but received no reply. Her captain tried again: "Are you in control?" Two more minutes of silence was followed by a badly garbled transmission at 9:17. The crew of the *Skylark* thought they could make out the phrase "exceeding test depth." Those were the last words ever heard from the *Thresher*. The only other sound picked up by the *Skylark* was a chilling one: a muted, dull thud — the sound of a ship breaking up.

Bucking the odds, the *Skylark* waited and hoped for some message from the *Thresher* at the time scheduled for her next routine report, 10:17. None came. At 11:04 AM the *Thresher* was reported missing.

At first the naval command took a wait-and-see approach. The commander of the submarine flotilla to which the *Thresher* was assigned said, "Underwater communications are unreliable, and there are many instances when we lose communications with submarines. . . . I have one of these incidents about once a week." By mid-afternoon, however, his tone was graver: "This doesn't look good."

The Navy launched a search and rescue mission, but the term "rescue" held little meaning this time. The top brass admitted that they simply didn't have any vessels equipped for a rescue in the depths where the *Thresher* went down. Still, for three days subs, destroyers, frigates and planes combed an area of 12 square miles surrounding the spot where the *Thresher* had dived. All they turned up were bits of cork and plastic floating in an oil slick.

Finally the Navy admitted what was already clear. The *Thresher*, with 129 on board, had been lost. It was the U.S. Navy's worst peacetime submarine disaster.

Some months later the mangled remains of the *Thresher* were discovered on the ocean floor by an exploratory sub the Navy had brought to the site. An investigation placed the blame on a failure in the *Thresher's* piping system which short-circuited a transformer and shut down the nuclear reactor. The submarine's stern started to sink and attempts to blow the ballast tanks failed. Powerless, the *Thresher* descended to the ocean bottom 8400 feet below and was crushed by the enormous weight of the water. The end, the Navy told the families of the dead, must have come quickly.

Still, this was all conjecture. Despite months of secret investigation, the Navy would never finally know what happened to the *Thresher*. "It's like a murder case," said one admiral, "without the *corpus delicti*."

The Disaster at Vaiont Dam – 1963

In 1963 Italy suffered one of the worst dam disasters in modern history, but it was a disaster with a bizarre twist. The dam itself remained rock-steady throughout.

The Vaiont Dam was part of a network of dams and reservoirs built in the Italian Alps in the early 1960s to provide electric power to the country. The Vaiont, said to be the third-highest concrete dam in the world, held back a man-made lake that stretched back four miles.

The fall of 1963 had brought weeks of rain to the Piave River Valley, where the Vaiont was located. Mount Toc loomed high over Vaiont's lake, and the rains were pounding away at it. In the two years since the dam had been in operation engineers and geologists had openly voiced concern that the mountain behind it was unstable. As the rain continued villagers began to feel uneasy. The mayor of one town posted signs warning of danger from the shifting earth on Mount Toc. Shepherds noticed that their flocks were unsettled and moved them to higher ground. At the end of September half of the people in a village just below

BELOW: *The Vaiont Dam in Longarone, Italy, pictured the day after a landslide into its lake forced millions of tons of water over the dam and down the narrow Piave Valley. The 300-foot wall of water wiped out whole villages in minutes on October 9, 1963.*

ABOVE: *Five days after the Vaiont Dam disaster, survivors search for possessions among the rubble. At least 1800 people were killed by the wall of water, and many thousands more were left homeless.*

the dam left en masse because of fears about the dam's safety. And just before 11:00 on the night of October 9, their worst fears were realized.

In the valley below the dam there was a terrifying roar: the sound of Mount Toc disintegrating. One hundred and fifty million tons of rock and earth slid from the mountain and into the lake behind the Vaiont Dam. The effect, said an engineer who inspected the scene, was like that of "a stone dropped in a teacup." Water from the lake leaped hundreds of feet into the air, and then millions of tons of pent-up water washed over the dam in a huge wave and went roaring down into the Piave River Valley.

Some residents of the 10 villages in its path managed to hurry to higher land. Most were not so lucky. Langarone, the biggest town in the valley, was hardest hit, losing almost its entire population to the wave of water that at one point reached to 200 feet. At least half a dozen smaller communities were also devastated. The destruction took just six minutes.

Survivors dug frantically in the mud, sometimes using no more than a spoon, to try to find their relatives. Many of the dead were never identified; whole families had been lost and no one was left to claim the bodies or report the missing. A firm death toll was never established. The official count was 1800, but there were some reports that said that as many as 2500 people had been killed.

Early news from the disaster site suggested that the dam had burst under the weight of all the water. But an inspection soon revealed that it had held firm. A court of inquiry subsequently discovered that engineers had had serious reservations about locating a dam under a potentially unstable mountain. Their fears had been heightened when Mount Toc began to crack and crumble during the construction of the Vaiont Dam. Like the St. Francis Dam, the Vaiont had been built where it didn't belong.

After thousands of Italian soldiers died there fighting the Austrians during the First World War, the Piave River Valley acquired a somber name: the Valley of Death. Nearly 50 years later, sadly, the Vaiont Dam disaster was to show that the name still applied.

The Aberfan Avalanche – 1966

For decades the landscape of South Wales has been blighted by hundreds of "tips," heaps of mud and rocks and slag. The tips are a kind of necessary evil, the grim by-product of the Welsh livelihood, coal mining.

In the 1960s, however, the people of the Welsh town of Aberfan were growing increasingly concerned about one of the slag piles positioned precariously on the side of a hill over the town. Over the course of about 70 years the tip had grown hundreds of feet high, and some people swore that they had seen it shift ominously. Despite reassurances from the National Coal Board, Aberfan feared that the unstable mound was a disaster waiting to happen. It was October 21, 1966, when disaster struck.

Heavy rain had fallen for the past few days, and the tip, already weakened by an underground spring, had grown increasingly water-logged. Finally the pressure of all the water was simply too much. With a sound like thunder the base of the tip burst open. Two million tons of mud spilled out into the valley below, heading toward the center of Aberfan, a half-mile away.

At the local school the children had just said their morning prayers when the tip began to slide into the valley. Miners who had seen it collapse raced towards the school, which was directly in the path of the mudslide, but in seconds the building was engulfed. A youngster late for school that day watched as two friends disappeared before his eyes. "It looked like water pouring down the hillside. . . . It just sucked them away. . . . It hit the school like a big wave, spattering all over the place and crushing the building. It was like a dream, and I was very scared."

Mothers rushed to the school to try to find their children. Soon over a thousand miners converged there as well, shovels in hand and ready to dig. It was a heartbreaking task. One man carried the bodies of three children, including one of his own, from the school, then fell to the ground. "Their work was on the wall," he moaned. "A tot had drawn a picture of a zebra going across a road. 'Safe crossing,' it said, 'Safe crossing.'" Other rescuers came across a teacher with his arms around five children, as if to protect them. They were all dead.

A woman who climbed in one of the school windows managed to lead 12 youngsters out to safety. But her next attempt left her shaken. "We went to another classroom which was terribly damaged, and we could hear the voice of a girl but we could not get to her because there were other children trapped nearby, and if we moved anything, it would have collapsed on them. We could not rescue that little girl who said her name was Katherine. I have been thinking of Katherine all day and wondering whether she was saved or is still there."

The mud avalanche took 144 lives in the small village of Aberfan, and 116 of them were children. "A whole generation has been wiped out," one resident mourned.

The people of Aberfan lost no time in assigning blame for the disaster. "Buried alive by the National Coal Board" was the bitter rallying cry of the victims' families at the official inquest. The Welsh had long ago learned to live with tragedies in the mines themselves; those came with the territory. But they would not allow their children to be victims too. In the wake of the deaths they pushed hard for change, and succeeded in securing measures that would see to it that a disaster like the one in Aberfan in 1966 would never happen again.

TOP LEFT: *Mud flowed through windows of a school at Aberfan in South Wales, after tons of coal pit waste engulfed the village on October 21, 1966. Perched on a hill above the town, the enormous slag pile collapsed with the weight of a heavy rain.*

LEFT: *The day after the mudslide, a bulldozer pushes back slag from the Pantglas Secondary School in Aberfan. The Junior School was worst hit.*

TOP: *Women wait in anguish for word of the children who were in Aberfan's school that was engulfed by tons of coal pit waste. Of the 144 deaths caused by the tragic slide, 116 were children.*

ABOVE: *The day after the disaster, men, women and children of Aberfan make a sandbag barrier to prevent another slide from ravaging their town.*

The Peru Avalanche – 1970

Much of Peru had settled in for the afternoon on Sunday, May 31, 1970, to watch the televised World Cup soccer match between Mexico and the Soviet Union. Peru was also a contender, and soccer fans there were keeping close track of the matches. But in the closing moments of the game the country found itself facing a disaster that made soccer seem of little consequence.

At 3:24 that afternoon, along the Andes Mountain chain, the earth began to shake to a degree Peruvians had never before felt. The worst earthquake in South American history, measuring 7.7 on the Richter scale, was underway. Thoughts of soccer were abandoned as people rushed into the streets to seek safety from the falling buildings. But worse was to come.

High over the towns of Yungay and Ranrahirca in northern Peru Mount Huarascan was disintegrating. Ice and rock cascaded in a 10,000-foot free-fall from the west side of the mountain, then gathered speed until it was racing down the valley at nearly 500 miles per hour. Part of the slide landed in a mountain lake, causing it to overflow

and transform the ice and rock avalanche into a giant mudslide. By the time the wave reached Yungay and Ranrahirca 10 miles down the valley it was a raging mass of ice, rocks and mud that buried the two towns alive, killing almost all who lived there. A reporter flying over the scene days later described it as nothing more than a vast expanse of mud, "like a face whose features had been wiped away."

Closer to the Pacific coast, the industrial and fishing city of Chimbote, one of Peru's bright hopes, also lay in ruins. No avalanche had buried it, but the earthquake alone had destroyed three-quarters of the city. In Chimbote, the same reporter observed, "I felt as though I were seeing a town through which a careless giant had walked, crushing homes at every step."

Lima, Peru's capital, had also felt major shocks, but the city at first had no inkling of how much devastation the quake had caused less than 200 miles away. Early government estimates of the dead were modest – just a few hundred. But within hours it was clear that Peru had experienced a major disaster. The country's president

LEFT: *Indian residents of Ranrahirca, Peru, walk along a mud-covered street on January 13, 1902, three days after an avalanche destroyed most of the village and wiped out several other villages, claiming more than 3000 lives. Disastrous as it was, this landslide was only a small indication of what was to come.*

ABOVE: *An overturned, mud-covered bus lies at the site of what was once the Plaza de Armas in Yungay, Peru. This city of 20,000 – and Ranrahirca – was wiped out by the May 31, 1970 avalanche triggered by the worse earthquake in South American history. Almost 70,000 people died.*

headed for Chimbote to assess the damage and ended up bringing several hundred of the injured back to Lima for treatment. Medical facilities in the hardest-hit spots were in ruins.

Rescuers were at a loss as to where or how to begin their work. Much of the affected area was buried in mud, and roads were impassable. Thousands of people who initially survived the earthquake and avalanche died from lack of food and shelter. There were instances in which the injured managed to drag themselves to the nearest town, sure they would get help there, only to find it in worse shape than the place they'd come from.

The 1970 Peru earthquake and avalanche erased dozens of towns and villages from the landscape, and caused property damage in the billions of dollars. When the final death count was in, it was staggering. Nearly 70,000 Peruvians had died. The 1970 earthquake still stands as the worst in modern South American history.

The Bangladesh Cyclone – 1970

Set at the mouth of the Ganges River facing the Bay of Bengal, the area that is now Bangladesh is one of the most vulnerable spots on earth, an easy target for the bay's killer cyclones. The majority of Bangladesh's people live on the silty islands of the delta, one of the few spots in the country where food crops will flourish. But the low delta lands that are so fertile are heartbreakingly susceptible to flooding. People go there to grow food, but they live with the knowledge that their good fortune can last only until the next big storm swirls into being over the Bay of Bengal.

An 1876 cyclone there killed 300,000, and one in 1942, 40,000. In 1963, 22,000 more died from cyclones, and in 1965, another 55,000. But when a ferocious storm struck Bangladesh – then still East Pakistan – in November 1970, historians had to go all the way back to 1737 to find a cyclone that rivaled its destruction.

As the second week of November began weather satellites began tracking a massive storm forming over the bay. Radio warnings were broadcast, but most people in East Pakistan had no radios, and those who did discounted the reports since a much advertised storm a few weeks earlier had not amounted to much. The ferocity of this new cyclone, however, would make the issue of whether adequate warning was given almost irrelevant.

The moon was full and tides were high on November 12 as the cyclone's winds whipped through the Bay of Bengal toward East Pakistan. High waves began to pound the offshore islands. Then the heart of the disaster struck. Late that night people reported hearing a roar (as if it were the end of the world, they said) and seeing a glow that came

LEFT: *Some of the dwellings in Kachha, on the coast of Bangladesh, are completely destroyed by the cyclone and tidal wave that devastated the area on November 12, 1970.*

BELOW, FAR LEFT: *A large steamer from Chittagong was tossed into a field on Bangladesh's Manpura Island by the raging waters that accompanied the cyclone of 1970.*

BELOW LEFT: *A rescue party prepares to bury the body of a dead child in Charjabber – one of the victims of the cyclone that claimed over 300,000 lives in Bangladesh.*

BELOW: *Bangladeshi soldiers unload relief supplies from an Italian aircraft at Dhaka's airport.*

nearer and nearer. Propelled by rising tides, pelting rain and heavy winds that were now reaching 150 miles per hour, a wall of water surged over the delta, carrying away everything in its path – people, animals, houses, crops. Some reports said that the tidal wave towered 20 feet over the land; others said 50 feet.

When the storm subsided the scene might well have been the end of the world. The 1970 cyclone ranks as one of the worst disasters in all of human history. Bodies were everywhere, dangling from trees, floating in the muddy streams, washing up on beaches. At least 300,000 people died, most by drowning, but the estimate is almost surely too low. Some news reports said that 500,000 died; others contended that even a million deaths would not be exaggeration.

Further devastation awaited those who managed to survive. The promise of food that had drawn millions to the river delta was no more. Over a million acres of rice paddies were gone, and so were a million head of livestock. There was almost no drinking water. Despite aid from around the world, many thousands more were fated to die from starvation and disease.

The cyclone of 1970 was to have a profound effect on the politics of East Pakistan. The union with the rest of Pakistan, to the west of India, had long been an uneasy one. Now, embittered by the lack of help its own countrymen offered, the people of East Pakistan rebelled in a bloody civil war for independence. A year after the cyclone had devastated its land and its people, East Pakistan was reborn as the nation of Bangladesh.

The Wankie Mine Explosion – 1972

United Nations sanctions had placed Rhodesia (now Zimbabwe) in a precarious economic state in the early 1970s, forced to resort to the black market for much of its trade. The country's only coal mine, the Wankie Colliery, was one of the few bright spots in the struggle to stay afloat economically. The coal itself was not exported, but it was vital to Rhodesia's rail lines and industry.

Most of the workers at the Wankie mines were from other African nations, recruited by the mine company with lures of good housing, schools and sports facilities. Early in June of 1972 the government announced that the Wankie Colliery's labor supply was now plentiful enough to man the mines for the foreseeable future. The very next day an accident occurred that was to undermine that work force critically.

Equipped with the most up-to-date equipment, Wankie's Number 2 shaft was the most productive in the mine. But on June 6 workers above ground were startled by the sight of one of the mine's cable cars shooting out from the shaft with enough force to propel it a full 50 yards from the mine entrance, injuring several people on the surface. The cable car signalled a much worse disaster below ground. In the sloping shaft's long tunnel, there had been a mammoth explosion, and over 400 miners were trapped.

All through the day and night rescue workers struggled to reach the miners. But the shaft quickly filled with a deadly mix of methane gas and carbon monoxide. For 15 hours the rescue crew persevered. Finally, when it was clear that the mounting quantities of gas were placing the rescuers in danger too, the mine company temporarily halted their efforts. Near the entrance to the mine shaft groups of African women swayed back and forth and wailed in mourning for the trapped men.

The mine company decided to try another tactic. By pumping oxygen into the shaft they could drive the poisonous fumes down deep, permitting access to the upper portions of the mine. Authorities had by now conceded that there was no hope of finding anyone alive in the Number 2 shaft; the task of the rescuers was to recover the dead. Still, as they headed deeper and deeper into the shaft the rescue team listened for the "pipe talk" that miners employ to show that they are still alive, trapped fortuitously in a pocket of air. In the Wankie mine there was no such sound.

Three days after the explosion the chairman of the company announced that there was "no cause for hope." The missing, he added, "died instantly and were not aware of what had happened."

The Wankie explosion was one of the worst mining disasters on record. A 1942 coal dust explosion in a Manchuria colliery had taken more than 1500 lives. In 1906 over a thousand miners died in Courrières, France. But those accidents were years ago. The Rhodesian mine had some of the best technology available. In spite of that, the final death toll released on July 4 reported that 427 miners had lost their lives in the Wankie explosion.

Almost a year later, the inquiry commission which investigated the accident issued its report. The explosion, it stated, was due to a build-up of methane gas. The report censured the Anglo-American Corporation of South Africa for "a serious neglect of duty" in failing to detect the presence of the deadly gas.

LEFT: *An aerial view of Rhodesia's Wankie Colliery after an underground explosion trapped 427 miners, June 6, 1972.*

RIGHT: *This photo reveals the Wankie Colliery's main ventilation shaft after it was blown out by the fatal explosion caused by a build-up of methane gas.*

BELOW: *While rescue efforts are attempted, rows of stretchers laid out on the ground wait for the miners trapped in the Wankie Colliery.*

Hurricane Fifi – 1974

Perhaps it was her name that made the hurricane heading toward the Central American nation of Honduras in September of 1974 seem so tame. How much threat could a storm called Fifi pose? Hurricane Carmen had passed by Honduras just a couple of weeks earlier, and despite the drama that name conjures up, the country had barely been touched by the storm. No one expected Hurricane Fifi to be any different.

Those with an eye for details might have noted a curious cycle in Honduran history, however. In 1914, in 1934 and again in 1954 the country's north coast had been swamped by floods. Could 1974 bring more of the same?

It wasn't until Fifi roared in on the Honduras coast on September 19 that she came into her own, dumping 20 inches of rain in less than 40 hours. Rivers that had been little more than trickles were suddenly raging torrents that washed away entire communities. In the market town of Choloma, people woke at 3:00 in the morning to the sound of a deluge of water that had spilled from one of the now-mighty rivers nearby. Said a survivor afterward, "It was like a wild thing." Water-borne debris washed through Choloma, killing nearly 3000 people and burying the town under as much as 12 feet of mud.

Fifi attacked the core of the struggling Honduran economy, devastating the 6000-square-mile region that was the agricultural and industrial heartland. Beans and coffee just ready for harvest were washed away. The banana crop, Honduras' main export, was nearly a total loss, with damages to it reaching $112 million. Tarantulas flushed from the banana plantations by the water added to the Hondurans' misery.

When Fifi departed, Honduras' transportation was in shambles, and it was days, and in some places weeks, before relief workers could reach many of those in need. One family clung to high-tension wires for four days to keep above the flood waters before help arrived.

ABOVE: *Houses in a banana plantation near San Pedro are surrounded by muddy waters in the aftermath of Hurricane Fifi.*

LEFT: *Survivors in Choloma, a town which suffered 3000 casualties from the hurricane.*

ABOVE RIGHT: *A satellite photo shows Hurricane Fifi heading westward below Cuba on September 18, 1974.*

RIGHT: *In the aftermath of Hurricane Hugo, which struck the area on September 22, 1989, pleasure boats are jammed together in a pile at South Carolina's Isle of Palms.*

More heavy rains a few weeks later compounded the difficulty of the relief effort. As late as November 30,000 people were still stranded in one part of Honduras, dependent on only the supplies that could be airlifted in to them by helicopter.

There have been other Atlantic hurricanes responsible for far more damage than Fifi: Camille in 1969, Agnes in 1972. Hurricane Hugo, in 1989, was one of the costliest storms ever, causing some $4 billion in losses. But in terms of human lives claimed, none compares to Fifi. Soon after she struck, the Honduran government released a report that put the death toll at 2000. But Fifi had destroyed half of the nation's food supply, and fallout from the storm continued well in 1975. Some sources contend that Hurricane Fifi eventually brought about the deaths of as many as 8000 Hondurans.

The Sao Paulo Office Fire – 1974

Sao Paulo, Brazil, was a city on the rise in 1974. Its population was booming, and so was its skyline; statistics showed 60 new buildings being completed every 24 hours. The 25-story Joelma Building, a combination parking garage and office building, was one of the city's newest skyscrapers.

Sao Paulo had plenty of civic boosters proud of the city's up-to-the-minute architecture. What it did not have, tragically, was a bureaucracy concerned with such unglamorous aspects of development as fire safety.

More than 500 people, many of them employees of an investment bank housed in the Joelma Building, were already at work on the morning of February 1 when a fire broke out in a 12th-floor air conditioning unit. Several hundred people on the lower floors managed to get downstairs to safety. Another 70 or so above the fire made their way through flames and down the stairs. But the rest, it would soon be evident, had no exit. The fire spread upwards within minutes, trapping dozens of workers.

Sao Paulo's fire department, only 1300 strong for a city of eight million, was all but powerless to rescue them. Skyscrapers are beyond the reach of traditional firefighting equipment such as hoses and ladders. Instead the buildings rely on fireproof materials and design features to prevent the spread of fire from floor to floor. In the Joelma Building, however, there was no fireproof stairwell, no fireproof barriers between floors and no adequate alarm system. Furthermore, the designers of the sleek new building had inexplicably used flammable plastics throughout, turning the skyscraper into a high-tech tinderbox.

As the flames grew hotter around them, the people on the upper floors became desperate. Rescuers on the ground tried to stem a wave of panic by holding up signs reading, "Calm," "Wait" and "Danger is past." Unable to get to the trapped workers with their ladders, which reached less than halfway up the building, firefighters managed to rescue some by ferrying them across a rope to another building. But for most people the danger was clearly not past, and they knew it. As the fire grew more ferocious some clung to window ledges until their strength was gone, then dropped to their deaths. Others flung themselves from the windows as the heat became more than they could bear. A crowd of some 10,000 spectators gathered to watch the grisly spectacle.

Several dozen people managed to reach the roof of the Joelma Building, where they waved frantically at rescue helicopters hovering overhead. But the heat was so intense that the craft could not land – there was concern that their fuel tanks might explode. It was not until the fire was under control several hours later that the helicopters finally picked up the rooftop survivors.

It took firefighters four hours to quell the blaze. When it was over, the upper half of the brand-new Joelma Building was a charred skeleton. The fire had taken its toll in the first 25 minutes: 189 dead, either killed by falls from the building or turned to ashes by temperatures of nearly 1300 degrees Fahrenheit. The deceptively modern Joelma Building, in the end, was a state-of-the-art death trap.

LEFT: *People trapped on the roof of Sao Paulo's burning Joelma Building reach out to a rescue helicopter as flames rage through the building. Intense heat prevented the helicopters from landing for some hours, at which point several dozen people were picked up.*

RIGHT: *Beyond the reach of rescuers and desperate to escape the blaze, an unidentified man leaps to his death from the Joelma Building. The fire claimed 189 lives.*

The Chinese Earthquake – 1976

Back in 1556 China had suffered through the worst earthquake in recorded history, and in the years since then the country had endured damage from hundreds more quakes. The leaders of the People's Republic of China vowed to address the problem in a new way, with an earthquake prediction system that would make use both of modern science and ancient folk wisdom.

Scattered throughout the country were 5000 data-gathering stations. Some of the data consisted of precise seismological measurements of such phenomena as the movement of geological fault lines. But just as important was the information collected by so-called "barefoot seismologists," ordinary people who kept track of the signs that the Chinese had relied on for centuries to predict when an earthquake might hit – the color of well water, for instance, or the way the animals were behaving. A 1973 pamphlet distributed by the government suggested that the lay observers keep an eye out for these harbingers of an impending quake: "When rabbits with their ears standing jump up or crash into things, when fish jump out of the water as if frightened."

The system had shown itself to be effective in 1975 when officials evacuated Liaoning Province just before a quake hit the region. But the following year, in 1976, the government's new warning system failed.

It was just before 4:00 in the morning on July 28 when one of China's most densely populated regions was jolted by an earthquake that measured 8.2 on the Richter scale. Sixteen hours later another tremor struck, with an intensity of 7.9. Asleep in their houses at the time of the first earthquake, thousands of Chinese were easy prey.

In Peking the tremors were severe enough to crack plaster and shatter windows, and the people headed for the streets, where they were to stay for the next two weeks; Chinese officials feared a series of aftershocks and had warned people to stay out of buildings. Peking turned into a tent city, with citizens returning to their homes only to wash and, if they were brave, to sleep. At foreign embassies, diplomats camped out in courtyards and on tennis courts. The precautions were prudent: 15 aftershocks measuring 5 or higher on the Richter scale were recorded.

But for all its appearance of a city in distress, Peking had barely been touched compared to the industrial and mining city of Tangshan, about 100 miles to the southeast. The government was close-mouthed about the extent of the damage there, but a French visitor to the city at the time of the earthquake reported that it was "ruined totally, 100 percent." Tangshan, a city of one million people, was gone. A full year after the quake, a visitor likened it to the site of an atomic bomb blast.

The Chinese regard such cataclysms of nature as omens, and are reluctant to reveal much about them. Thus it was weeks before a death toll was reported. When it was, it stunned the world: more than 655,000 people had died. Many Chinese feared that the 1976 quake boded still more ill for their country. One U.S. publication noted, "Even in the reborn China of Mao Tse-Tung, a quake as immense as the one in Tangshan has a specific meaning to the superstitious. It foreshadows, they believe, the impending death of an emperor."

That report was published on August 9, 1976. One month later to the day, on September 9, 1976, China's legendary leader, Mao Tse-Tung, died.

LEFT: *A partial view of the ruined Chinese city of Tangshan reveals the great extent of the damage done by the earthquake that struck on July 28, 1976.*

BELOW LEFT: *For weeks after the earthquake rocked China's most populous region, residents of Peking camped outdoors. Tremors continued until mid-August.*

BELOW: *One of 25,000 who were killed in the earthquake that devastated Armenia on December 7, 1988. The severity of the quake brought China's calamity, 12 years earlier, to mind.*

BOTTOM: *A series of earthquakes hit Mexico City on September 19, 1985, causing 3000 deaths. Here survivors survey the damage.*

The Zagreb Mid-Air Collision – 1976

The air corridor that passes over central Europe is one of the world's most crowded, and aircraft are layered carefully into the available space. At low altitudes, under 29,000 feet, air traffic controllers make sure there is at least 1000 feet of vertical separation between aircraft flying in opposite directions, and in the upper reaches of the sky, where the fastest jets travel, that margin of safety is upped to 2000 feet. If everyone goes by the rules there is room for all. But on September 10, 1976, the rules were broken.

On that day a British Airways Trident jet was en route from London to Istanbul. Going in the other direction was a DC-9 charter from Yugoslavia bringing a group of West German tourists home from a two-week holiday on the Adriatic coast. The British jet carried nine crew members and 54 passengers; the DC-9, five crew and 108 passengers.

Near the city of Zagreb in Yugoslavia the pilot of the DC-9 requested permission from the ground to climb over its assigned altitude. Such requests are routine, and air traffic controllers are authorized to grant them once they determine that no other traffic is already in that space. The controller on the ground in Zagreb radioed his approval, and the DC-9 began its climb. Its pilot could not know that another plane, the British Airways Trident, was already at the same altitude, and flying directly toward the Yugoslav jet.

Down at 29,000 feet, a Lufthansa pilot was winging his way along the same corridor when something caught his eye. He looked up to witness the Trident and the DC-9 closing in on each other from opposite directions. A moment later they collided head-on.

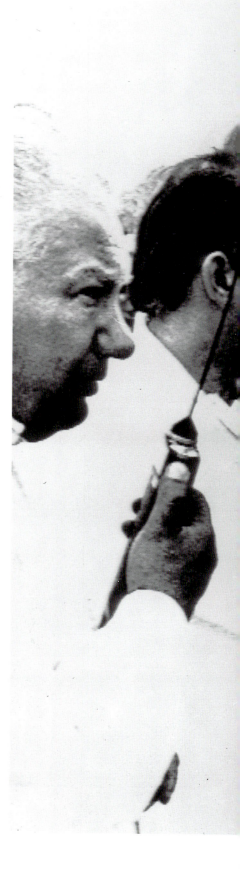

RIGHT: *Officials inspect the wreckage in Belgrade after British and Yugoslavian airliners collided, killing all 176 aboard both planes and scattering debris over eight miles of Yugoslav countryside. The tragic collision, which was ruled to be the fault of the air traffic controllers, took place on September 10, 1976.*

BELOW: *An earlier airplane crash littered a Yugoslavian suburb with shattered metal. On October 30, 1975, a Yugoslav DC-9 crashed near Prague Ruczyne airport, killing 68 of the 120 on board.*

Bodies and luggage and chunks of metal spilled from the sky, scattering over eight miles of Yugoslav countryside. The DC-9 burst into flames and disintegrated on impact with the ground, but the Trident managed to survive the crash in nearly one piece. Its passengers were beyond hope, however.

A policeman who was among the first to arrive on the scene found one small baby still alive, but it died before medical help reached the crash site. All 63 on board the British Airways flight and all 113 aboard the Yugoslav jet were killed. It was the worst mid-air collision in history.

Immediately after the accident the speculation began. Was there a malfunction in the altimeters of one or both of the jets? Did the pilots misunderstand the directions from the air traffic controller? Or had the controller simply failed to do his job of maintaining the 2000-foot buffer zone in the airways?

In the end a Yugoslav investigation placed the blame for the accident on the controllers. Eight of them were charged with a variety of breaches of procedure, but when the trial was over only one was convicted, on charges of criminal negligence and criminal responsibility for all 176 deaths. The court ruled that the controller had granted the DC-9 permission to climb to an altitude that set it on a collision course with the Trident; when he discovered his error, the controller had still failed to act. It was the first time in the history of civil aviation than an air traffic controller had been convicted of criminal negligence. He was sentenced to seven years in prison for causing the deaths of 176 people.

The Canary Island Airport Collision – 1977

The Romans and Greeks had a special name for the welcoming cluster of islands off Africa's northwest coast: "The Fortunate Islands." But Spain's Canary Islands became the site of utter misfortune on March 27, 1977, for the passengers and crew aboard two jumbo jets at the Los Rodeos Airport on Tenerife.

Pan Am Flight 1736 from Los Angeles was filled with older Americans heading to Las Palmas to board a cruise ship; KLM Flight 4805 carried Dutch tourists looking forward to spending their Easter holiday in the Canary Islands' sun. The flights of the two 747s had gone smoothly until air controllers radioed a change in the flight plans. A bomb explosion in the airport flower shop had shut down the major airport in the Canary Islands at Las Palmas, and the Pan Am and KLM flights were both diverted to the small Tenerife airport as a safety measure until Las Palmas reopened.

The two jets landed routinely and then awaited word that they could proceed to Las Palmas; the KLM craft took advantage of the time on the ground to refuel.

Heavy fog on the two-mile runway had reduced visibility to just over 1500 feet when word came that Las Palmas had reopened. Following the tower's orders, KLM captain Jacob Veldhuizen Van Zanten eased his craft down the single runway to a holding position in preparation for takeoff. The Pan Am jet, captained by Victor Grubbs, was told to follow three minutes later and turn off at the third intersection to await its turn for takeoff. Clear instructions, but as it happened, not clear enough.

There were four intersections on the runway, and their layout proved confusing to the Pan Am crew. The first turn-off was blocked by other aircraft, and the Pan Am crew considered it inactive. The third intersection angled away from the runway so sharply that a jumbo jet would be hard-pressed to maneuver into it. The crew concluded that the controller wanted them to head for the next intersection.

In the meantime, the KLM jet had been told to stand by for takeoff and await further word from the tower. Pan Am was instructed to radio when it was clear of the runway, and the crew acknowledged the message. Pan Am Flight 1736 was just 475 feet from its exit when its crew saw lights approaching through the fog. "We are still on the runway!" Grubbs radioed the control tower. His message was too late. The KLM jet was heading toward him at full throttle, its huge mass bearing down at 186 miles per hour.

Desperately, Grubbs yanked his craft to one side. At the same time, the KLM captain struggled to pull his jet's nose into the air. Both efforts were futile. The KLM 747 slammed into the Pan Am jet, ripping off the top of the fuselage from just behind the cockpit all the way to the tail and sending it toppling onto its side. The KLM skidded to a halt 1500 feet down the runway. In seconds, its just-filled fuel tanks exploded, creating a 2000-degree inferno that turned both planes into giant fireballs.

The result was the worst air disaster in history: 582 people dead. All 249 on board the KLM jet were killed; of the 394 passengers and crew on the Pan Am craft, 333 died. The 61 survivors had been seated in the front section of the plane.

The enormity of the disaster was made even more staggering by the irony surrounding it. The crash occurred on the ground, at an airport that had been serving as a haven for the rerouted airliners. There was no mechanical failure involved. While there was heavy fog, pilots knew how to deal with that, and no other fluke of wind or weather had played a role. The captain of the KLM jet, Van Zanten, was one of the line's most experienced pilots, featured in that month's in-flight magazine as living proof of KLM's reliability.

In the end, though, a Spanish board of investigation placed the major share of the blame on KLM. Its captain, they determined, had made the most basic of mistakes: he had ignored the control tower's instructions and taken off without clearance. He and 581 other people paid a high price for that mistake.

BELOW: *Skeletal remains of a 747 frame the wreckage after the fiery ground collision between KLM and Pan Am jumbo jetliners at the Canary Islands' Los Rodeos Airport at Tenerife claimed 583 lives.*

RIGHT: *The charred tail of a passenger jet looms before Tenerife's control tower as soldiers prepare to remove the wreckage. The Canary Island collision of March 27, 1977, was the worst air disaster in history.*

BELOW RIGHT: *Morticians work on a crash victim in a makeshift morgue in a hangar at Tenerife.*

The *Amoco Cadiz* Oil Spill – 1978

As she made her way from the Persian Gulf to Lyme, England, in 1978 the supertanker *Amoco Cadiz* was carrying a full load: 1.6 million barrels of light crude oil. On March 16 the *Amoco Cadiz* began to spill that precious cargo – and defile a shoreline.

The tanker had run up against heavy seas and high winds along France's rock-strewn Brittany coast, and when a problem developed in the vessel's steering mechanism it was clear she was headed for trouble. The *Amoco Cadiz* summoned a tugboat to steer her clear of the rocks, but the rough seas snapped the tow line, and the ship was left to founder. A French naval helicopter picked up the crew from the ship, save for the captain and a safety officer who chose to remain aboard. The safety officer described the tanker's final throes as she crashed on the rocks and finally broke in two: "The stern sat solid, but the bow was twisting and heaving in front of us. Then she broke her back, with a screech of metal and a shower of sparks that lasted 10 minutes."

The accident involved more than the loss of a ship. It let loose millions of gallons of oil. Day by day the oil seeped into the water. Engineers tried to seal the tanks but failed; so did attempts to transfer the *Amoco Cadiz*' cargo to other tankers. The gradual leakage made it hard to mop up the oil, so authorities decided it would be best to release all of it at once by detonating depth charges to blast the tanks open. Again they met with failure. By March 22, when the last of the ship's holds gave out on its own terms, over a million barrels had already spilled. The sea between France and England was an oily wasteland, with the oil a foot thick in some spots.

The effect on the area was devastating. Brittany boasted a picturesque coast popular with tourists from all over Europe, but now the prospect of sunning themselves on oily beaches kept the tourists away. The fishing industry in Brittany supplied France with a third of its fish; that, too, was a victim of the spill. Eighty percent of the year's oyster harvest was destroyed, and 90 percent of the seaweed harvest, which was prized by the chemical industry. The effect on wildlife was just as dramatic. Thousands of sea birds died in the oily muck.

Onshore cleanup efforts started at once. Bretons took up pails and shovels and headed for the shore to mop up what they could. Inflatable booms trapped some of the oil, and styrofoam blocks were used to soak it up. But the cleanup was a Sisyphean task. No sooner was an area clean than more oil would wash up on it. Said one oceanographer, "The technology for cleaning up oil lags far behind the technology for carrying it." France quickly instituted new safety regulations regarding tanker transport near its coast. And at the beaches, Bretons posted signs reading, *La mer est morte* – "The sea is dead."

All 1.6 million barrels of oil on board the *Amoco Cadiz* eventually leaked from the ship. The spill was the worst ever caused by the grounding of a single tanker, far greater than the *Exxon Valdez* spill off Alaska in 1989. Shortly after the wreck of the *Amoco Cadiz*, a marine biologist predicted that it would be seven to 10 years before the coastline recovered. He was an optimist. A 1985 report on oil spills singled out the *Amoco Cadiz* disaster. It might be decades, the report said, before the Brittany coast returned to pre-1978 conditions.

LEFT: *Seven days after she first began to founder off the Brittany coast on March 16, 1978, the Amoco Cadiz supertanker remains broken and leaking in the water.*

ABOVE: *Spilled oil from the Amoco Cadiz is cornered in a small bay at Roscoff village on the French coast. Tanker trucks bring detergent to break up the oil.*

RIGHT: *The oily bow of the wrecked supertanker rides the waves off Portsall, France. All 1.6 million barrels of oil she carried would eventually leak into the sea.*

LEFT: *Oil from the stricken tanker, the Exxon Valdez (left) is pumped aboard the Exxon Baton Rouge as cleanup efforts continue in Alaska.*

ABOVE: *Leaking since hitting a reef on March 23, 1989, the* Exxon Valdez *is towed.*

RIGHT: *A sea otter snacks on some clams in the oily waters of the Port of Valdez, after the disastrous oil spill.*

BELOW: *Workers at Valdez attempt to wash oil from the rocks into the water, where it can be contained and skimmed up.*

The Ixtoc Oil Spill – 1979

The Ixtoc I oil well off Mexico's Yucatan Peninsula had one purpose: to discover just how much oil was waiting to be tapped under the sea. On June 3, 1979, its operators found, there was more oil than they could handle. The well blew, soiling the Bay of Campeche and later the Gulf of Mexico with millions of barrels of crude oil.

A glitch in the routine drilling on June 3 led to the blowout that turned Ixtoc into a runaway well. Gushing at a rate of up to 50,000 barrels each day, the oil quickly formed a slick 100 miles long and 10 miles wide. A scheme to cap the well and clean up the mess was in the works almost immediately. But the job would confound oil spill experts called in by Pemex, the Mexican oil agency, and take much longer than anyone expected.

The experts had no shortage of strategies. They set a controlled fire at the spill site to consume some of the oil. They used oil recovery boats to skim up to 5000 barrels each day from the water. From above, airplanes dropped chemicals into the gulf to disperse the oil into smaller sections. Oil booms were also in place.

But it wasn't enough. By the end of August the flow had been staunched some, but Ixtoc was still a runaway well. Nearly two million barrels of oil had been released, and clumps of oil were appearing along the Texas coastline, worrying fishermen and tourist officials.

Pemex realized it was time to try something different. In October workers managed to place a huge cone – a sombrero, it was called – on top of Ixtoc I. In theory, the sombrero would trap 85 percent of the oil that was still

gushing out into the bay. But despite the sombrero, the oil kept coming. Two relief wells were planned to lessen the pressure on Ixtoc I, but drilling the wells did not turn out to be an easy task, and the projected completion dates were pushed back further and further. Next Pemex tried injecting over 100,000 heavy metal balls into Ixtoc I.

The spill continued on into the next year. In January of 1980 as many as 5000 barrels of oil a day were issuing from the well. It wasn't until March that engineers finally succeeded in capping Ixtoc I by filling the well with mud and then topping it off with quick-drying cement that formed a 685-foot plug.

The spill was the largest ever recorded, an estimated 3.1 million barrels by the time it was finally subdued. Fortunately, environmental damage was minimal, despite initial fears. But the Ixtoc blowout highlighted the inadequacy of oil technology. Man could tap vast supplies of oil beneath the ocean. But if it slipped away, he was ill-equipped to clean up after it.

Another set of concerns also manifested itself in the wake of the Ixtoc blowout. Pemex had dealt with Texas oil companies in the operation of the well, and the spill presented thorny legal dilemmas: When a spill involves more than one country, who is responsible for the cleanup? Who pays compensation for damages?

For Mexico, though, the disaster did at least bring some good news along with the bad. The runaway well had demonstrated that the Ixtoc field held vast stores of oil – perhaps as many as 800 million barrels.

OPPOSITE TOP: *A map showing the path of the oil slick two months after the Ixtoc I oil well blew on June 3, 1979, spewing one and a half million gallons of oil a day.*

OPPOSITE BOTTOM: *Workers on a platform douse the blazing runaway Ixtoc I well with water on August 2. The drilling platform (right) would later drill a relief well in an attempt to stifle the gusher.*

ABOVE: *A scientist pokes at the oily sludge that coats a beach at Puerto del Mesquital, 30 miles south of the Mexican border.*

RIGHT: *Natural gas flares above the surface after a 310-ton cone was placed over the Ixtoc I well on October 16. The "sombrero" did not staunch the release of oil.*

The Bhagmati River Train Wreck – 1981

The train that ran between Samastipur and Banmankhi in the state of Bihar, India, was packed on Saturday, June 6, 1981. Crowds of people were heading home from a day spent at the markets, and because it was the marriage season, there were a number of large wedding parties on board as well. The weather was poor that day, so far fewer people than usual were riding on the train's roof, a practice common in India. Instead, they had jammed inside the train's passenger cars. Built to seat just 54, on June 6 the coaches may have been holding as many as 200 people each. No one knows for sure how many were aboard Train No. 416.

Despite its "express" designation, the train made a number of stops along its route to take on and discharge passengers, adding to the confusion about the number on board. It was a typical Saturday run, except for the increasingly turbulent weather. When the train left Badla Ghat and failed to show up at the next station, just 14 minutes away over the Bhagmati River bridge, the stationmasters grew concerned. Down the track near the bridge they could see smoke from the train's locomotive. Half an hour later, people ran into the Badla Ghat station telling of a terrible train accident.

As it passed across the river, Train No. 416 had been buffeted by a hailstorm accompanied by powerful winds. The engine and first two cars of the train had made it across easily. But the rest, seven more cars, had tumbled into the Bhagmati River. Two of the cars jutted out above the surface, but the other five had disappeared beneath the muddy water.

LEFT: *Boatmen tow a victim's body to shore after the Bhagmati River train wreck killed between 500 and 800 passengers on June 6, 1981. Seven cars of the crowded train fell off a bridge in Mansi, India.*

ABOVE: *An aerial view shows the wreckage of No. 416. The cause of the disaster – which was possibly the worst railroad accident in history – was never determined.*

Divers from the Indian Navy began an underwater rescue mission in the turbulent river. But visibility was so limited that it was days before the frogmen would locate all seven cars. One had been washed a mile downstream.

Less than 100 people were taken from the wreck alive. The divers entered the churning waters over and over to break into the submerged cars and managed to recover 269 bodies. But many bodies were never found. In all likelihood dozens of people had been swept far down river. There were reports that one official offered local fishermen $6 for each body they found.

Judging from the number of people crowded into the cars that hadn't fallen into the river, authorities knew that far more than 269 people had died in the derailment of Train No. 416. The true death toll was probably at least 500, and possibly as many as 800.

The cause of the accident sparked a bitter debate in India. On the one hand, the government claimed that the hailstorm the train had encountered had spawned a sudden cyclone-like wind that had lifted the cars from the tracks and sent them plunging down into the Bhagmati. From the state's point of view, the accident was due to an unavoidable act of nature. But others who had been at the scene reported that the train crew had braked suddenly to avoid hitting a bull on the track, and, in fact, an injured bull and the body of its owner were found near the accident site. To subscribers to this version, the state-run railway was at fault. The issue was never resolved.

The number of confirmed deaths alone made the Bihar train derailment one of the worst railroad accidents on record. When the hundreds more who almost surely drowned but were never found are considered, the Bhagmati River accident may well be the worst railroad accident in history.

The Australian Brush Fires – 1983

In the early 1980s Australia was in the grips of the worst drought it had experienced in this century. Some spots had not seen rain in four years, and by 1983 much of the country was dry as tinder. When gale-force winds began to blow over the southeast coast in February of that year the stage was set for one of the worst forest and brush fires on record.

It was on Ash Wednesday, oddly enough, that the brush fires began to spring up. It's unclear how all of them started, but with temperatures over 100 degrees Fahrenheit the parched vegetation was clearly ripe for fire. Man also had a hand, however, in at least some of the blazes. There were signs of arson at several spots.

However the fires started, they would soon merge into one massive firestorm. Winds of over 60 miles per hour drove the flames until they became a wall of fire charging through dry brush, eucalyptus forests, seacoast resort villages and farmland alike. Within hours of the first flicker, sheets of flames 50 feet high were racing along out of control.

People packed their families in their cars and drove off to try to outrun the fires, but many were not fast enough: thousands of Australians were trapped inside burning cars. The direction the fire would take next was unpredictable, making escape difficult. Thus a dozen volunteer firefighters battling the flames from trucks were killed when a sudden shift in the wind sent the fire back on them.

In the hilltop village of Macedon, a survivor described the onslaught of the blaze: "The fire came up the highway,

like a fireball. The roar of the wind and the flames was horrific, like a train." Two hundred people gathered in the local pub, their heads wrapped in damp towels to protect them from heat and smoke. They had picked the right spot to seek refuge; by morning, all that was left of Macedon was a telephone booth, the train station and the pub.

Four days after the first tiny fire had started the blaze was still burning along some parts of the coast. When it was finally over it had left hundreds of miles of Australia between Melbourne and Adelaide in ruins, with great clouds of ash hovering overhead. In all, over two million acres of land had been destroyed, half a million more than were burned in the great forest fires that raged in the western United States in 1988. What made the Australian fire even more devastating was that its path ran not just through forests and scrub land, but heavily settled areas as well.

Property damage was estimated at over $450 million and the death toll was 71, with thousands more injured. Said Prime Minister Malcolm Fraser as he viewed the destruction from the air, "A panzer division could not have done as much damage. There is nothing left."

Australians soon had a focus for their anger about what had become of much of their land. On February 18 two men were charged with arson for setting at least a portion of the fires that led to the conflagration. In court, the judge looked at one of them, a 19-year-old unemployed sheet metal worker, and summed up the feelings of his country. "You," he told the young man, "are probably the most unpopular man in South Australia right now."

LEFT: *Brush fires break out on the slopes of Australia's Mount Wellington, March 2, 1983. The parched conditions and strong winds created a massive firestorm that engulfed two million acres.*

RIGHT: *The fires in Australia – some of which were traced to arson – raged out of control.*

BELOW: *Forest fires devastated one and a half million acres in western United States in 1988 after drought conditions similar to those in Australia set the stage. Here an Army helicopter flies to a water drop in Yellowstone on August 31.*

BELOW RIGHT: *Attempting to stop the march of destruction through Yellowstone, a firefighter sets a backfire.*

The Bhopal Chemical Plant Leak – 1984

The pesticides produced at the Union Carbide plant in Bhopal, India, were especially potent tools in India's "Green Revolution" in agriculture in the 1980s. One, carbamate, could be used on 100 different crops against 180 insects, and it would do its work in less than 24 hours. On December 3, 1984, an accident at the Bhopal plant showed how lethal these pesticides were for human beings as well.

Shortly after midnight on that day a maintenance worker spotted a problem in the tanks that held methyl isocyanate, one of the chemicals used in the production of carbamate. The temperature was mounting precipitously, and pressure in the tanks was growing. By the time supervisors arrived on the scene it was too late: a white cloud of methyl isocyanate gas had begun to leak from the plant. The safety systems that should have prevented such an accident by neutralizing any overflow of gas inexplicably failed. And for the next half hour as much as five tons of toxic white gas drifted over the sleeping city of Bhopal.

Weather conditions were cool, calm and misty – just right, tragically, to allow the cloud to settle over a 25-square mile section of the city. Some victims died immediately, but almost 200,000 people, by one account, went screaming from their homes. Their eyes were burning, they could not breathe and red foam was frothing from their mouths. Some victims thought they had been bombed, others that the city was in the sudden grip of a plague.

Within hours nearly 2000 people were dead. Most succumbed to massive asthma attacks triggered when the air passages in their lungs filled with the poisonous gas. Others suffocated when the gas caused their lungs to fill with fluid. Fifty thousand more people suffered injuries. Some had serious lung damage, but there were also cases of liver damage and blindness.

Indian health officials soon had additional worries. Thousands of animals had also been killed by the leak; their rotting carcasses were drawing rats, vultures and dogs and were posing a serious threat of epidemic. Huge pyres of bodies were soon burning in Bhopal.

The Bhopal leak was the worst industrial disaster the world had yet seen, and both Union Carbide and India's state government came under attack. Safety standards at the Bhopal plant, it was charged, were less stringent than those at Union Carbide's North American facilities. A company official denied that, but he did admit that the Indian plant was without a computerized warning system like the one at the U.S. site that produced methyl isocyanate. Indian officials were criticized for even allowing Union Carbide to build in such a densely settled area as Bhopal, which had a population of 800,000. In fact, the plant had been built in an undeveloped region, but its construction brought in thousands of workers who soon created settlements approved by the government.

In three days all traces of the gas had dissipated from Bhopal. But the effects of the accident were to be far-reaching. The official death toll would eventually mount to 2352, but the true figure is probably well over 3000. Survivors were suffering from chronic eye and lung problems, miscarriages and stillbirths, and mental illness. A year after the accident, 65 major lawsuits had been filed, and the tangle of litigation resulting from the gas leak promised to clog the courts for years. For Bhopal's victims, of course, the consequences of the accident would last a lifetime.

LEFT: *The closed entrance to the Union Carbide plant in Bhopal, India, which leaked a cloud of toxic gas over the city on December 3, 1984, claiming at least 2352 lives.*

BELOW LEFT: *Women affected by the accident at Bhopal line up with doctors' prescriptions to receive free medicine at a clinic.*

RIGHT: *Children play with water near the body of a cow killed in Bhopal's lethal gas cloud. The thousands of animals killed by the leak posed a serious health threat.*

BELOW: *A year after the disaster, patients still crowd the 50-bed ward at the state-run Hamidia Hospital in Bhopal.*

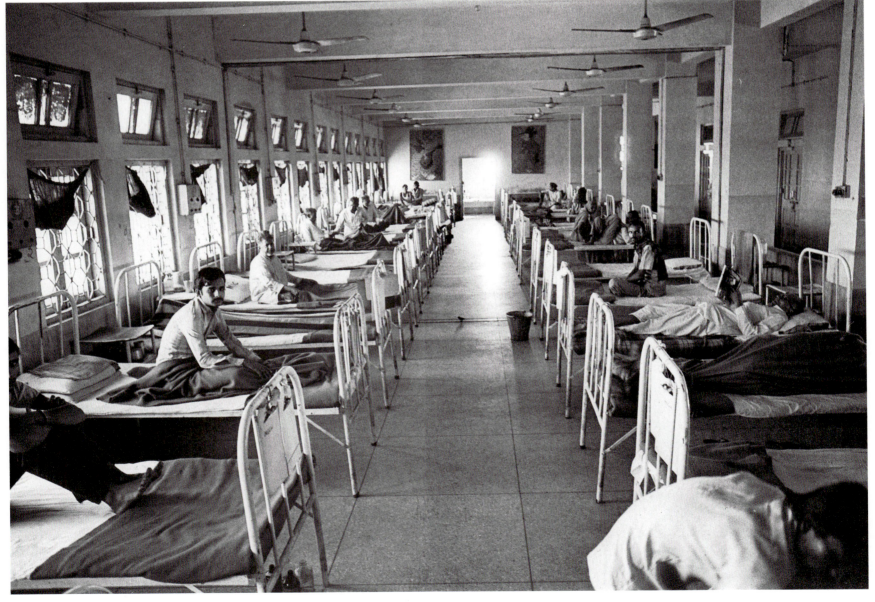

The British Soccer Disasters – 1985, 1989

With crowds frequently erupting into hooliganism, the 1980s had not been the best of times for soccer in England. Then a different kind of trouble, a fire at a stadium about 200 miles north of London, dealt the sport an even worse blow.

Ten thousand fans were on hand in Bradford City to watch the home team play Lincoln City on May 11, 1985. Something beneath the wooden grandstand section – a lighted cigarette, perhaps, or a smoke bomb in a soda can – ignited the piles of litter that had been tossed there by spectators. Then, said the coach of the Bradford team afterwards, "The fire simply erupted at the back of the stand and seemed to spread everywhere inside seconds."

As television viewers watched in horror, tall flames fanned by a stiff breeze engulfed the wooden grandstand, where 3000 fans were seated. Dozens of adults and children, hair and clothes ablaze, ran from their seats to try to escape the fire. But the grandstand's rear exit was locked. Some people ran onto the field and rolled about trying to smother the flames.

The blaze claimed 56 lives and left more than 200 injured. The grandstand had burned to the ground in minutes. Afterwards it was revealed that the city council had repeatedly warned stadium officials that the stands posed a fire hazard.

Four years later, just 30 miles away, another disaster was to shake English soccer once again and claim even more lives. The 54,000-seat Hillsborough Stadium in Sheffield had been chosen as a neutral site for an important match between Liverpool and Nottingham on April 15, 1989. In the wake of a number of incidents of rowdyism that had caused English teams to be banned from European competition, officials were working to defuse potentially dangerous fan confrontations.

The Liverpool-Nottingham kickoff was set for 3:00 PM. Shortly before game time more than 4000 fans were still waiting at the entry to the standing-room only section, far too many to pass through the turnstiles in the few minutes remaining. As the crowd grew increasingly unruly stadium authorities abandoned hopes of admitting them in an orderly fashion and threw the gates open wide. The result was a stampede. Fans rushed in, pushing up hard against the spectators who were already tightly packed inside.

Dozens of people were trampled underfoot or had the breath squeezed out of them when they were pinned against the fence separating fans from the field. Their agony was visible to the world in newsphotos that showed contorted faces mashed into chain link fencing. Many of those killed were youngsters who had gone up front for a better view.

Fans tried to escape the bedlam by climbing the fences and spilling out onto the field. Incredibly, play in the game continued. Finally, in the sixth minute, officials grasped the extent of the terror in the stands and called off the match. Gates to the field were opened so that the injured could be laid out on the grass for medical care.

European soccer has claimed dozens of lives in recent years, but never on the scale of the Sheffield disaster. When the bodies were counted, 95 people had died in the crush of fans, and 200 more had been injured. Once again, England was forced to step back and reflect on a troubled national sport – one that no longer seemed so sporting.

LEFT: *Fire rips through the grandstand at Bradford City soccer ground on May 11, 1985. Fifty-six people died in the fast-moving blaze.*

BELOW LEFT: *Mourners pay tribute to the 95 people who died two days earlier – on April 15, 1989 – at Hillsborough Stadium in Sheffield.*

BELOW: *England's neighbor, Belgium, also suffered soccer-related tragedy on May 30, 1985, when a crowd surge at the European Cup final caused a wall to collapse, killing dozens of people.*

BOTTOM: *Police and others help fans over the fence at Hillsborough Stadium.*

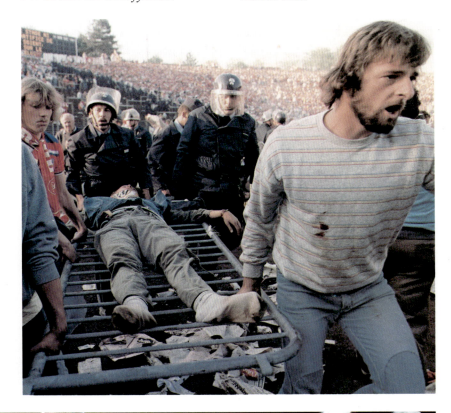

The Japan Air Lines Crash – 1985

The Japan Air Lines run from Tokyo to Osaka was a short hop, covering 250 miles in just under an hour. At 6:12 on the evening of August 12, 1985, the jumbo jet was filled to the limit, with 509 passengers and 15 crew members, as it began another routine flight from Tokyo's Haneda Airport.

Thirteen minutes after takeoff, however, it no longer had the makings of a routine flight. The cockpit relayed a message to ground control: "Immediate . . . trouble. Request turn back to Haneda." Two minutes later the Boeing 747 began transmitting an electronic emergency signal.

An off-duty crew member who was on the flight, Yumi Ochiai, was startled by a loud noise. Looking back in the cabin, she saw that part of the ceiling was missing. The cabin was filled with a white mist due to the drop in air pressure, and oxygen masks dropped down.

At 6:28 the air controllers again had contact with the JAL flight. Once more they heard a troubling message: "Uncontrol." By now the plane was rolling violently from side to side as the captain tried to steer by alternating power to his engines. When Ochiai saw Mount Fuji from the window she realized that the plane was radically off course.

The crew radioed to the controllers again at 6:46, "Uncontrol." A minute later, the same message: "Uncontrol-

lable." The 747 was losing altitude steadily. Its assigned air space was 22,000 feet, and it was now flying at less than half that altitude.

At 6:49 the controllers heard a frightened cry in the jet's cockpit – the first expression of fear. Five minutes later Haneda airport advised the JAL crew of its position. "Roger," came the reply. That was the last heard from the jet. At 6:57 PM, after 45 minutes of struggling to stay airborne, the 747 disappeared from Haneda's radar screen.

In the isolated village of Nippara a man looked up and saw a plane dropping from the sky, "flying just like a staggering drunk." It crashed in flames high on a remote mountain.

Trapped in the wreckage, Yumi Ochiai heard children's cries that grew weaker and weaker – and the sound of a helicopter flying over. Then she drifted off to sleep. In the helicopter the crew surveyed the burning plane and despaired of finding survivors. Without a place to land they headed back to a spot below the mountain where a rescue camp was being set up.

After that initial fly-by it was to be nearly 14 hours until help reached the crash site. Some rescuers traveled on foot through the mountainous terrain. Others were airlifted in and lowered by rope. There to retrieve the bodies

of the dead, they were stunned to find four people still alive: a mother and daughter, another young girl and Ochiai.

Those four survived, but the 520 who died made the JAL crash the worst single-plane disaster in history. Afterwards physicians said that if help had arrived earlier more lives could have been saved.

Hundreds of relatives had gathered at the base of the mountain, and some managed to make their way to the burned-out plane. A mother and father knelt at the seat that had been assigned to their 9-year-old son, who had been on his way to visit an uncle.

The day after the crash a piece of the 747's tailfin was recovered from the bay near Tokyo. Investigations soon focused on the bulkhead section of the craft. Damage to it in a minor accident some years earlier, plus the stress of frequent takeoffs and landings, investigators felt, caused the bulkhead's blowout and loss of the tailfin.

The five other JAL crashes in the previous 13 years had all been attributed to pilot error. This time, that couldn't have been further from the truth. Aviation experts around the world agreed: the pilot had shown extraordinary skill in keeping his jet in the skies as long as he did.

LEFT: *After constructing a helicopter landing site, workers continue cleanup operations after a Japan Air Lines Boeing 747 crashed onto Mount Osutaka near the village of Nippara, on August 12, 1985. With a death toll of 520, the tragic crash was the worst single-plane disaster in history.*

ABOVE RIGHT: *A Japanese Self-Defense Force troop lifts one of the four airplane crash survivors, 12-year-old Keiko Kawakami, to a rescue helicopter at the site of the disaster.*

RIGHT: *A piece of the downed 747's hull is lodged, amidst debris, in the forest where the plane crashed and burned. Rescuers were slow to respond, reaching the site 14 hours after the crash; more lives would have been saved if help had come more quickly.*

The Eruption of Nevado del Ruiz – 1985

When the Colombian volcano known as Nevado del Ruiz showed its first signs of life in 1984 after nearly four centuries of silence, the Colombian government began mapping out a disaster plan in case of an eruption. The plan warned of potential slides caused by melting ice and mud from the snow-capped peak that rose over 16,000 feet into the sky. But there was no need for alarm, the authors of the study reassured those who lived in the volcano's shadow. "The mud moves very slowly," they said, slowly enough to permit an orderly evacuation.

The experts were correct in predicting an eruption, but they were terribly wrong in their sanguine view of the consequences. On November 13, 1985, a smell of sulfur began to drift through the air in the valley below Nevado del Ruiz. From deep in the earth came a mighty rumble. And then, as steaming magma forced its way upwards, Nevado del Ruiz erupted in a spectacular flash. The heat was intense enough to singe a plane flying 25,000 feet above the volcano. On the ground, recalled a survivor, "the whole world began to scream."

A hot, dirty river of rocks, mud and water surged down into the valleys below Nevado del Ruiz. There was clearly no time to allow any evacuation, let alone a leisurely one. In Armero, a town of 20,000 people, a survivor recalled that the avalanche "rolled into town with a moaning sound, like some sort of monster." Buildings, with the people still in them, were buried beneath as much as 15 feet of mud. The town's mayor died in his home as he tried to radio for help.

In another spot the onslaught of the avalanche woke a 19-year-old pregnant woman from her night's sleep. With her husband, daughter and mother she headed into the street and began trying to outrun the wave of mud. It caught up with them in just one block, mighty enough to knock her daughter from her husband's arms. The woman sank beneath the mud. When she surfaced, the town was dark. Then she was swept away, to be rescued finally by a cab driver. There was no trace of her family.

Armero was hardest hit, but the avalanche also buried parts of at least a dozen other communities. Rescue workers had to battle quicksand-like mud to try to fish the injured from the wreckage. Days later, a cloud of ash still hung darkly over the entire area.

Contrary to the norm for most disasters, this one left far more people dead than injured. Just under 23,000 people died from the avalanche caused by the eruption of Nevado del Ruiz; only 4000 or so were injured. The casualty figures made it clear that anyone unfortunate enough to have been in the path of the volcano's river of mud was almost surely doomed. Another 22,000 people were left homeless, and damages came to $275 million.

Nevado del Ruiz had last erupted back in the time of the Spanish explorers. In the 1980s, with a disaster plan in the works, Colombia wished it had remained at rest for just a few more years. As a geologist noted with some irony, "The volcano erupted too soon."

GREAT DISASTERS OF THE 20TH CENTURY

LEFT: *The Colombian volcano Nevado del Ruiz, photographed a week after its violent eruption on November 13, 1985, triggered a landslide that claimed 23,000 lives.*

RIGHT: *A man weeps at the site of his former home in Armero after the avalanche killed all five members of his family. Directly in the path of the deadly landslide, Armero, with its 20,000 inhabitants, was practically wiped out.*

BELOW: *Survivors of the eruption and landslide make their way from Armero to landing sites where rescue helicopters will evacuate them.*

BELOW RIGHT: *An aerial view shows the destruction caused by the massive slide of rocks and mud that swept through Armero after the eruption of Nevado del Ruiz.*

LEFT: *Washington's Mount St. Helens sends up steam after a major eruption on May 18, 1980. The volcano devastated a large area, causing 60 deaths.*

ABOVE: *Red Cross workers carry a survivor from Armero, Colombia, to a waiting helicopter, in which he and others will be taken to medical facilities.*

RIGHT: *Trees were laid flat from the force of the blast when Mount St. Helens erupted in 1980. The volcano has been active several times since then.*

The *Challenger* Explosion – 1986

By 1986, the 25th anniversary of manned space flight, the American public had grown so accustomed to one successful mission after another that launches merited little more than a mention in the day's news. But the space shuttle launch set for January of that year was different. The *Challenger* was to have a special passenger accompanying its crew of six: teacher Sharon Christa McAuliffe – the first teacher in space – on board to beam back science lessons to America's schoolchildren as she circled the Earth far above them.

The air at Florida's Cape Canaveral was unusually cold on the morning of January 28. The launch, which had already been scratched on four previous occasions, was now delayed for several hours due to mechanical problems and ice. But the *Challenger*'s send-off was to be carried live on television so children across the country could see their new classroom head into space, and NASA, the U.S. space agency, was itching to get *Challenger* airborne.

Finally, at 11:38, there was lift-off. The *Challenger* arced into the sky as 24 shuttle missions before it had. But just 73 seconds into its flight NASA would be dealt its most severe setback.

The craft was 10 miles high and eight miles down from the launchpad, traveling at 1977 miles per hour, when an orange flame flickered from the base of the external fuel tank, which at lift-off had held a half million gallons of highly explosive liquid hydrogen and oxygen. In an instant the *Challenger* was a burning projectile in space. Moments later it broke up and plummeted toward earth, showering debris into the ocean for a full hour.

Mission Control was silent. Then came a report of a "major malfunction," followed by this terse notice: "A report from the flight dynamics officer that the vehicle has exploded." His voice cracking, the flight director came on: "The flight director confirms that."

America's momentum in space had come to a halt at a cost of seven lives and billions of dollars. It was both a national tragedy and a personal one. Family, friends and fellow teachers of McAuliffe had been at Cape Canaveral for the launch; now television showed their stricken faces. At Concord High School in New Hampshire, where McAuliffe taught, the excited chatter of students decked out in party hats and noisemakers turned to sobs.

At first the families of those lost on the *Challenger* could console themselves with NASA's reassurance that the crew had died at the moment of the explosion, with no inkling of their fate. But in July the agency released a tape on which Navy Commander Michael J. Smith, the *Challenger*'s pilot, said "uh-oh" at the precise time of the explosion. Clearly, he had known that something was wrong. Further evidence that the astronauts were aware of their situation came with the recovery of four air tanks; three of them had been turned on by hand.

A presidential commission appointed to investigate the shuttle accident placed the blame on faulty seals in the rocket boosters, a condition made worse by the frigid temperatures at launch time. But the commission went further, pointing fingers at two groups: NASA's middle management, for ignoring long-standing problems with the seals, and contractor Morton-Thiokol, Inc., for overruling its own engineers after they had argued heatedly with the NASA team the night before the launch about the safety of the seals.

The *Challenger* disaster produced major changes in United States space policy. NASA cancelled all shuttle flights until 1988 and rethought the goals of the shuttle program. No longer would shuttles be promoted as satellite launch vehicles to help pay their way financially. That would become the domain of private contractors. Instead, NASA would concentrate on scientific and defense missions for the shuttle. The lofty goals of the shuttle program had been scaled down, and the era of boundless optimism in the U.S. space program was over.

RIGHT: *The NASA space shuttle* Challenger *explodes 73 seconds after lift-off from Cape Canaveral, killing all seven aboard, including teacher Sharon Christa McAuliffe. The national tragedy caused a change in U.S. space policy.*

LEFT: *The crew of the* Challenger *heads for the van that will take them to the launchpad.*

ABOVE: *The official insignia for the* Challenger *mission. One of the mission's goals was observation of Halley's Comet. The apple symbolizes the first teacher in space.*

RIGHT: *With the* Challenger's *launchpad in the background, the flag flies at half-mast at the Kennedy Space Center.*

103

The Chernobyl Accident – 1986

The radiation measuring devices at one of Sweden's nuclear power plants on the Baltic Sea were showing that something was seriously wrong on April 28, 1986. At first technicians suspected a radiation leak at their own plant. But soon other nuclear power plants in Northern Europe were also reporting unusually high levels of radiation. Swedish officials announced that a nuclear accident had taken place, and pointed to the Soviet Union. The Swedes demanded an explanation.

At first there was silence from Moscow. But as world pressure mounted the Soviets conceded that there had been an accident at the Chernobyl nuclear power plant in the Ukrainian city of Pripyat, about 60 miles north of Kiev. The accident had resulted in just two deaths, according to the official announcement. Little else was revealed.

The USSR's secrecy about the nuclear accident was nothing new. Ever since 1959 there had been hints from Communist bloc scientists that a major nuclear event had occurred in the late 1950s in the city of Kyshtym. Entire villages were missing from maps of the area printed in the following years, and it is believed that the Kyshtym accident was responsible for many deaths. In 1976 a dissident Soviet scientist said he believed the accident involved the explosion of nuclear waste, and the subsequent contamination of a large area. Whether towns disappeared from maps because of widespread deaths or because they were evacuated is still not clear. The Soviet government has yet to disclose exactly what happened.

This time, however, there was no hiding the fact that another nuclear accident had occurred at a Soviet reactor.

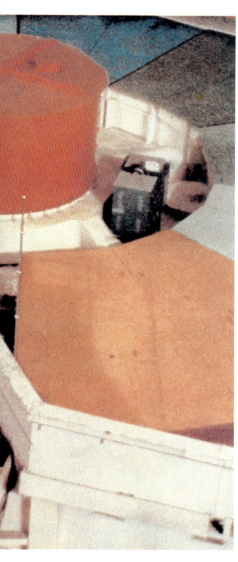

LEFT: *This photo from the February 1986 issue of* Soviet Life *magazine shows the cooling system of a nuclear reactor at the Chernobyl power plant near Kiev. Accompanying captions declared that "the control block of the plant can shut down the reactor in a matter of seconds."*

BELOW LEFT: *A helicopter flies past Chernobyl's damaged nuclear reactor after it exploded on April 26, 1986, sending radioactive fallout into the Ukraine and nearby countries.*

BELOW: *The head of the Pripyat fire brigade which fought the Chernobyl blaze points at a photo of the power station's damaged fourth reactor after the nuclear accident.*

In August, after pressure from other nations and from its own people, who had been bombarded by rumor upon rumor, the Soviet Union released details of the accident. There had been an explosion in one of the Chernobyl plant's four nuclear reactors during a test, resulting in a tenacious graphite fire in the reactor core. Western observers pieced together sketchy information and concluded that the accident was in all likelihood the result of poor plant design and lax safety procedures. The reactor fire burned for days, and the Soviets had eventually turned to Sweden and West Germany for help in putting it out.

In the weeks following the accident the USSR continued to insist that only two deaths had occurred from the explosion itself, and 29 more from radiation sickness. But enough radiation had leaked to warrant evacuation of 135,000 people in the 300 square miles around the plant. Over 200 people were treated for radiation burns.

The accident had an even broader range, however. Southeast winds pushed the radioactive cloud that rose from Chernobyl over much of Europe. In just a few days the cloud had drifted more than 1600 miles to the west. Crops, livestock and dairy products had to be destroyed because of radiation contamination.

The long-term effects of Chernobyl will not be known for years. Contaminated food and water will continue to pose an environmental hazard, and the thousands of Soviets who were exposed to radiation run a significant risk of illness sometime in the future. Over the next 70 years, say some scientists, up to 10,000 people may die from cancer caused by exposure to Chernobyl's radiation.

The Lake Nios Poison Gas Eruption – 1986

The Lake Nios area of the West African nation of Cameroon was famous for its robust cattle. So when a visitor from outside the farm community approached one day in August of 1986 and came upon one dead cow, then another and another, he knew that something was very wrong around Lake Nios.

At first he found only livestock strewn everywhere, but soon he discovered human bodies as well. The more he looked, the more the area around Lake Nios began to resemble a vast open-air charnel house. Yet despite the mass deaths – more than 1700 people, and thousands of animals, it turned out – the countryside was untouched. The villagers' huts stood as if nothing had happened.

"It was as though a neutron bomb had exploded," a rescue worker later observed. "Bodies everywhere – but the buildings were still standing."

What had happened was a freak of nature. The usually crystalline blue waters of Lake Nios had turned a muddy brown, offering a clue to the disaster: deadly gas had erupted from the lake late in the evening of August 21. Within minutes the gas had killed all who came in contact with it. Victims were found with their hands over their noses, trying to seal out the noxious fumes. Others had torn off their clothes in an attempt to escape the burning sensation caused by the gas, and had then collapsed a few yards away. In Nios, the community nearest the lake, only two people out of a population of roughly 1000 survived. In the nearby village of Su-Bum, which was equally devastated, rescue workers came upon a lone chicken poking among the bodies littering one family farm.

With no electricity or paved roads, the Lake Nios area was hard to reach, and it was several days before word of the disaster reached the world. When rescuers finally arrived there was almost no one left to rescue, so lethal was the gas. Instead they set about burying the dead. The official death toll was placed at 1746, but authorities conceded that the figure was probably low, since some survivors had buried their dead before help arrived.

What had caused Lake Nios suddenly to turn fatal? Experts began theorizing immediately, with most leaning toward one scenario. Lake Nios is a volcanic lake, set in a crater and deeper by far that most other lakes. Over the centuries, toxic gases, produced by both volcanic magma and rotting vegetation, had built up in the bottom of the lake. In most bodies of water these gases have plenty of escape hatches – faults in the earth, dissipation into the water. But Lake Nios' unusual depth kept the gases in check. It took some kind of disturbance – perhaps a landslide into the lake, perhaps an underground tremor – to upset the delicate balance. Toxic gases shot to the surface and then spread in a cloud over the countryside.

The cloud was made up of an undetermined mix of gases: probably carbon dioxide and hydrogen sulfide, possibly carbon monoxide and cyanide, too. It so enveloped the area that people who breathed it suffocated from lack of oxygen.

Rescue workers were struck by the eerie nature of the disaster at Lake Nios: human and animal life gone, yet homes with food on the fires and youngsters' toys scattered about, as if the occupants had just stepped out. One disaster relief expert called it a scene straight from Ripley's "Believe It Or Not." Another observer was more reflective. "The silence," he said, "is so deep."

BELOW: *Dead cattle sprawl on a hillside in northwest Cameroon after the toxic gas released from nearby Lake Nios on August 21, 1986, killed thousands of animals and at least 1746 people.*

BOTTOM: *The deserted village of Su-Bum near Lake Nios, whose inhabitants have fled or been killed by toxic gas.*

RIGHT: *Lake Nios turned from blue to a muddy brown color after an underground tremor caused the release of lethal gases – produced by magma and organic decay – that had built up under the water.*

BELOW RIGHT: *Cameroon troops wear masks or noseplugs as they arrive at Su-Bum to bury victims of the tragic gas eruption.*

The *Dona Paz* Ferry Collision – 1987

Christmas 1987 was just five days away, and the Philippine ferry *Dona Paz* was overflowing with passengers looking forward to holiday reunions with their families in Manila. Crowded onto tiny cots, children listened as their mothers told them of the sights they would see and the aunts and uncles they would meet. All was calm on the night of December 20 as the ferry made its way through the waters of Tablas Strait, just 110 miles south of Manila.

Then, around 10:00, the passengers felt a sudden jolt, and the peaceful night turned into one of terror. With no warning that anything was amiss, the *Dona Paz* had collided with an oil tanker, the *Victor*. In moments the tanker's oil-filled holds exploded, turning both ships into torches and covering the sea with flames.

On the *Dona Paz'* lower decks the people were trapped in a maze of corridors with little chance of escape. Passengers on the upper levels faced a grim choice: how they wished to die. If they stayed on the ferry they would be burned alive. If they jumped into the sea they would almost surely burn in the oil that was fanning out over nearly one square mile, or else be eaten by the sharks that cruised the waters. Many chose to jump and were never seen again. A survivor later told how there had been a chorus of children's voices calling out from the sea, "Nanay!" (Mother!) and "Tatay!" (Father!).

Rescue ships managed to pull just 26 survivors from the strait that night, most of them badly burned. Of the *Victor's* crew of 13, only two survived. The *Dona Paz'* manifest listed 1583 passengers and 60 crew, but the handful of survivors said that the ferry had been jam-packed, perhaps to twice its capacity. The many people who had purchased their tickets at the last minute were not on the passenger list, nor, it was suspected, were perhaps a thousand young children.

The cause of the collision was never established. The *Dona Paz* did not maneuver to avoid the *Victor*, leading to speculation that the ferry had mechanical problems. The moonless night had made visibility minimal, and there was talk that the *Dona Paz'* navigation systems weren't operational, a condition that would not have been surprising in light of what some felt was slipshod enforcement of maritime safety regulations by Philippine authorities. Still others hinted that the fault lay with the officers of the ferry. The captain had reportedly been watching TV, and the first and third mates were relaxing with glasses of beer, leaving the bridge in the hands of an apprentice seaman. But this was merely conjecture. Everyone in a position to know the real cause of the accident had perished.

For decades the loss of the *Titanic* had been the worst peacetime maritime disaster in modern history. Now, 75 years later, an event occurring on the other side of the world had caused the *Titanic* to relinquish that title. In this case, however, there was no band playing to bolster the spirits of the people doomed to die; no stars of society on board; no gleaming decks; no glamour to transform a terrible end into a legend. On December 20, 1987, off the Philippines, there was only the stark fact that 3000 lives had been lost.

OPPOSITE: Dona Paz, *the ill-fated ferry that collided with an oil tanker on December 20, 1987, is shown on one of her previous voyages.*

RIGHT: *Another ferry disaster on a much smaller scale had occurred across the Atlantic earlier in 1987, when the* Herald of Free Enterprise *car ferry capsized off Zeebrugge, Belgium, on March 5, claiming 135 lives.*

BELOW: *Two days after the sinking of the* Dona Paz, *a worker loads victims' bodies onto a ship in Pinamalayan, Philippines.*

BELOW RIGHT: *Villagers retrieve victims of the* Dona Paz *disaster from the waters off Mindoro, Philippines.*

The Ramstein Air Show Crashes – 1988

LEFT: *A file photo depicts the 10-jet* Frecce Tricolori *display team. The spectacular formations and feats performed by the slick-flying team made it a popular air show attraction, until the disastrous crash at the air show in Ramstein, West Germany, on August 28, 1988.*

RIGHT: *Spectators run as one of the three Italian jets that collided at the Ramstein air show explodes in a fireball when it hits the ground. More than 400 people were injured, and 70 were killed in the tragic crash.*

BELOW RIGHT: *The twisted and charred wreckage of an Italian MB-339A aircraft lies on the ground at Ramstein, where it crashed into a crowd of spectators and exploded.*

With sleek jets and daring pilots from the top military aerobatic teams in the world, the air show at the United States Air Force Base in Ramstein, West Germany, on August 28, 1988, promised to be a spectacular day of entertainment.

A handful of demonstrators had picketed the base before the show, carrying signs that read "Stop the air shows. We're afraid," a reference to the crashes of several low-flying NATO jets in West Germany earlier that year. But the protesters were clearly outnumbered. The Ramstein Air Show had been an annual event since 1955, and this year 300,000 people were on hand. Families spread out their picnic gear and settled in to enjoy a day of precision flying at its finest.

Thousands of pairs of eyes were looking up into the sky as the 10-jet Italian team known as the *Frecce Tricolori*, or "Tricolored Arrows," sped through their dazzling repertoire. The team began a maneuver known as "The Heart." In it, nine jets were to fly in a line, then split and trace a heart in the sky as they trailed red, green and white smoke. The tenth jet would be the arrow flying through the heart. It was a flashy crowd-pleaser, one of the team's standard routines, and not especially difficult. But on this day the precision flying was not precise enough.

The first nine jets outlined the heart according to plan, and the tenth roared in toward the center. But as it did so, it clipped the wings of two of the other jets. All three jets tumbled from the air.

At first, some spectators recalled later, they thought it was all part of the show, but within seconds it became clear that it was not. One jet crashed into the woods, and another onto the tarmac. But the third jet, the one that was to have pierced the heart, plunged down into the thick crowd clustered around the concession stands, creating a fireball that towered 150 feet into the air.

Dozens of spectators died almost instantly from the intense fire. Others, their skin charred, stood stunned, as if in a daze. Food vendors took ice from their stands and applied it to the burned, and calls went out in the crowd for donations of blood for the injured.

It had been a family crowd at the air show that day, and many of the dead were children. When the final count was completed, 70 people had died at Ramstein, including the three Italian pilots. Over 400 more spectators were injured.

What went wrong? Videotapes of the Italian team showed the landing gear of the tenth jet extended, which was not standard procedure. Some observers thought the pilot who was to fly through the heart came in too low and too early. Others thought the opposite, that he was flying too slowly.

Whatever the cause, the Ramstein disaster was the worst in air show history, and the fact that it was carried into thousands of homes live via television made the horror even more immediate. The accident deeply disturbed West Germans and prompted an international debate. Were air shows, which not only entertained but served to drum up support for the military's newest planes, worth the risks they posed?

Index

PICTURE CREDITS

All of the photos in this book are courtesy of UPI/Bettmann Newsphotos with the exception of the following:
©All-Sport Photographic Ltd: 95(bottom).
Australian Overseas Information Service: 90, 91(top).
Brompton Photo Library: 101(bottom).
Cine Foto Bucci: 50(bottom), 51.
Public Archives, Nova Scotia: 29(bottom).
Stars and Stripes, Ireland Edition, Dec. 1943 – July 1944: 50(top).

ACKNOWLEDGMENTS

The author and publisher would like to thank the following people who have helped in the preparation of this book: Barbara Thrasher, who edited it; Adrian Hodgkins, who designed it; Rita Longabucco, who did the picture research; and Florence Norton, who prepared the index.